a god who mat

The Bardic Mysticism of Amergin
Including a New Translation of the Three Cauldrons Text
By: Christopher Scott Thompson

I am a god, who fashions smoke from magic fire for a head- Amergin

ISBN #- 978-1-304-45726-4
© 2013 Christopher Scott Thompson. All rights reserved.

Dedicated to Cicely, Leila, Rowan
and
Great Bríd of the Horses

The Legend of Amergin

Everyone with an interest in Irish mythology knows the story of Amergin, primeval bard of the Gaelic people: how he was the son of the great warrior king Mil from whom the Milesians were named, how the Milesians sailed to Ireland and did battle with the pagan gods and fairy host of the Tuatha de Danann, how he promised to name Ireland after the three goddesses Banba, Fodla and Eriu, how he gave the judgment that the Milesians must leave Ireland and sail beyond the ninth wave before returning to do battle, how the Tuatha de Danann attempted to keep the Milesians from landing but Amergin overcame them with a magical song invoking Ireland, and how he brokered the peace treaty by which the Tuatha de Danann retreated underground into the hollow hills and became the Sidhe people, while the Milesians went on to become the Gaels.

What most people don't realize is that this version of the story has been cleaned-up considerably from the original text, which makes a lot less sense because it is a bizarre mishmash of pre-Christian Irish lore, Biblical characters, pseudo-genealogy and outright fiction. Here are just a few of the confusing points in the original version.

Most accounts describe the god Nuada of the Silver Hand as being one of the Tuatha de Danann. In the *Book of Invasions* section 55-64, Nuada is a king of the Tuatha de Danann, but in 65-95 he is an ancestor of the Gaelic Irish or Milesians. In fact, the text says "every princely family that is in Ireland, save the Eoganacht, is of the seed of Nuadu Airgetlám."

In the *Book of Invasions* section 55-64, the Fomorians or "those from beneath the sea" are the enemies of the Tuatha de Danann. In other sources, the Fomorians are depicted as a race of misshapen giants. They are also the eternal enemies of the gods, the Gaelic equivalents of the Titans, Jotuns or Asuras of other

Indo-European mythologies. In sections 65-95 of the *Book of Invasons,* the Fomorians and the Tuatha de Danann are the exact same thing, and the Tuatha de Danann have giants fighting for them.

We are usually told that the Tuatha de Danann are the Irish gods while the Milesians are mortals, but in Amergin's magical poetry he refers to himself as being a god. If the Fomorians are giants and the Tuatha de Danann are gods and the Milesians are mortals, why are the Tuatha de Danann described as Fomorians and why are some of the Milesians described as being gods or as being descended from members of the Tuatha de Danann?

The fact is that the *Lebor Gabala* or "Book of Invasions," is neither myth as such nor history as such but a medieval pseudohistory written for a very specific purpose. The fili or poet-seers of early medieval Ireland worked for the ruling kings and chiefs of the various Irish tribes, but those rulers derived their authority from the pagan gods or deified ancestors they claimed to be descended from, such as Nuada of the Silver Hand.

In a newly Christianized Ireland, it was necessary to give them new genealogies derived from Biblical figures such as Noah, while retaining some connection to older native lore to avoid invalidating their previous claims and undermining their legitimacy. The *Book of Invasons* is not a collection of pre-Christian Irish legends about the history of the country, but an awkward attempt to graft random bits of pre-Christian lore onto the Biblical narrative to give the Irish rulers a place in the Christian world.

You can see this even in the names of the different tribes that supposedly conquered Ireland. The ancient Irish couldn't have called themselves the Milesians as in the *Lebor Gabala*, because the word "Milesians" is of Latin origin. It derives from Miles Hispaniae or "soldier of Spain," the supposed father of Amergin,

Eber Donn and the other Milesian leaders.

So, even though the *Lebor Gabala* contains an origin story in which the ancestors of the Gaelic aristocracy invade Ireland and drive the Tuatha de Danann underground into the Sidhe mounds with Amergin's help, we can be just about certain that there never was any pre-Christian Irish myth to this effect. Amergin's story in its current form is not a myth, it's a fiction.

That doesn't mean Amergin is not a mythic or pre-Christian figure. His name literally means "Birth of Song," so he is supposed to be the primal bard or fili. It is very possible, one might even say probable, that a primal bard called "Birth of Song" figured in the pre-Christian mythology of the Gaels. A number of the characters in the "Book of Invasions" are thought to have been pre-Christian deities or mythic figures. The authors of the book could have simply borrowed Amergin from whatever his original context was and fit him into their story about the fictional Milesian invaders, just as they did when they took the pre-Christian Irish god of the dead and turned him into Amergin's brother Eber Donn.

We can go a step further and speculate that the original pre-Christian version of this legend was not about human invaders at all, but a story about how the great bardic god Amergin tamed and harnessed the powers of the underworld. There are many details in the surviving lore about Amergin that hint at such an interpretation.

For one thing, his famous "Song of Amergin" begins with three lines invoking the power of the sea, and the Fomorians are "those from beneath the sea." Later in the same poem, he mentions the Fomorian sea-god Tethra and Tethra's "cattle," the fish of the ocean. He also describes himself as one who "seven times sought the fairy mounds without fear." Here is one version of Amergin's song, although you should bear in mind that the original text is highly obscure and different translators have almost completely different interpretations of some lines:

I am the wind on the sea (for depth);
I am a wave of the deep (for weight);
I am the sound of the sea (for horror);
I am a stag of seven points (for strength);
I am a hawk on a cliff (for deftness);
I am a tear of the sun (for clearness);
I am the fairest of herbs;
Í am a boar for valour;
I am a salmon in a pool (i.e. the pools of knowledge);
I am a lake on a plain (for extent);
I am a hill of Poetry (and knowledge);
I am a battle-waging spear with trophies (for spoiling or hewing);
I am a god, who fashions smoke from magic fire for a head (to slay therewith);
(Who, but I, will make clear every question?)
Who, but myself, knows the assemblies of the stone-house on the mountain of Slieve Mis?
Who (but the Poet) knows in what place the sun goes down?
Who seven times sought the fairy-mounds without fear?
Who declares them, the ages of the moon?
Who brings his kine from Tethra's house?
Who segregated Tethra's kine?
(For whom will the fish of the laughing sea be making welcome, but for me?)
Who shapeth weapons from hill to hill (wave to wave, letter to letter, point to point)?
Invoke, O people of the waves, invoke the satirist, that he may make an incantation for thee!
I, the druid, who set out letters in Ogham;
I, who part combatants;
I, who approach the fairy-mounds to seek a cunning satirist, that he may compose chants with me.
I am the wind on the sea.

(From: *The Poem-Book of the Gael*, edited by Eleanor Hull)

In my opinion, the Tuatha de Danann were originally celestial deities, gods of the Sky realm, while the Fomorians were cthonic or underworld deities of the Sea realm. The distinction between these divine races is nowhere near as clear-cut as it might appear from later retellings, because many of the Danann gods are partly Fomorian or have Fomorian connections or cthonic aspects. In Celtic lore, the Sea realm and the realm of the underworld are identical. So, when Amergin invokes the power of the Sea to aid him in his battles with Fomorian/Danann "demons," as the *Lebor Gabala* calls them, he is demonstrating his mastery of the underworld powers. His claim to have repeatedly visited the Sidhe mounds without fear is of the same type. Amergin, the greatest of the bards, defines his greatness by his fearless familiarity with the underworld.

This interpretation of Amergin's legend fits in with the legend of another Amergin, a later bard from the Ulster Cycle who was one of the foster-fathers of Cuchulain. In a very strange story called "Does Greth Eat Curds?", this Amergin begins life as a mysterious mute boy who is also monstrously ugly and spends his days crouching in a mound of his own filth while his belly slowly grows to enormous size as if he was pregnant. When he suddenly starts talking at age fourteen, the poet Aithirne recognizes his potential power as a fili and tries to kill him to remove the threat of competition for the position of chief poet. Later, he becomes Amergin's foster-father and teaches him everything he needs to know. As bizarre as this story is, the themes make sense in the context of the older Amergin legends. This Amergin (a reincarnation?) is silent because his mind is elsewhere, in the darkness and silence of the underworld realm. When he returns to this world, his power is immediately evident and horrifying to those around him.

There are several other poems and short texts attributed to the original Amergin, including the famous *Cauldron of Poesy* or "Three Cauldrons" text of bardic lore.

Because the Christian references in the Cauldron text rule out the possibility that it was actually written by the pre-Christian bard Amergin, most people don't seem to consider it in the context of the other works attributed to this mythical figure. This only makes sense if we think of Amergin as a historical person to whom "authentic" texts can be attributed, but this position simply isn't tenable- the *Book of Invasions* itself is not a history, so why should we assume it preserves the work of a specific historical poet?

No, the Cauldron text wasn't written by a historical bard named Amergin- but neither was the "Song of Amergin" or any other text. Amergin is a persona or a name to whom certain categories of texts could be attributed. When a medieval fili wanted to present lore dealing with mysterious powers and esoteric concepts, he attributed it to Amergin. (Or possibly thought of himself as channeling Amergin somehow.) The Welsh bards did the same thing with their primal bard, Taliesin.

When we think of Amergin in this way and then examine Amergin's most famous poem from that perspective, we can see some interesting points of connection with the Cauldron text. Both works contain references to the sea and to horror. In the Cauldron text, Amergin describes himself as, "Performing many horrifying displays, vast seas of poetry for Eber Donn."

In the "Song of Amergin," Amergin proclaims "I am the wind on the sea... I am a wave of the deep... I am the sound of the sea." While a modern reader might be inclined to interpret these images in terms of the relaxing sound of ocean waves lapping gently on the seashore, the glosses to the "Song of Amergin" specify that the first line is "for depth," the second "for weight," and the third "for horror."

What does it mean to say that the phrase "I am the wind on the sea" is "for depth" or that the phrase "I am the sound of the sea" is "for horror"?

In the *Colloquy of the Sages,* Néde mac Adnai goes to the edge of the sea to seek the answer to a question, because "the poets considered that beside water was always a place of revelation..."[1]

In the Three Realms world-model of Celtic belief, the realm of the Sea is the same as the underworld. Néde mac Adnai seeks *éicse* or mantic knowledge at the edge of the Sea because the source of his knowledge is the cthonic realm. Amergin's displays of poetry for Eber Donn, the god of the dead, are like "vast seas" for the same reason. In "The Song of Amergin," the first three lines invoke the power of the underworld, not just the power of the ocean as such.

In fact, the lines "I am the wind on the sea... I am a wave of the deep... I am the sound of the sea," when read according to the glosses, could be expressed as "I go deep inward... I feel heavy... I experience numinous awe"- depth, heaviness and horror. These first three lines are not early nature poetry, they're a technique of self-hypnotism to induce a trance state!

When we look at the "Song of Amergin" this way, the poem starts to look less like a pantheistic identification with the natural environment and more like a series of mantras meant to provide the poet-seer with specific powers. The glosses simply tell us what each mantra is good for.

Interpreting the lines as mantras or incantations, here is one possible set of interpretations.

The mantra *am gaeth i mmuir* "I am a wind on the sea" is used to induce mystical introspection, the sense of diving deep down to the inner darkness of the primeval Sea and the realm of the dead.

The mantra *am tond trethan* or "I am a wave of the deep" is used to induce the sense of heaviness associated with self-hypnotism

---

[1] <https://listserv.heanet.ie/cgi-bin/wa?A3=ind0012&L=GAELIC-L&E=8bit&P=7756&B=--&T=text%2Fplain;%20charset=iso-8859-1> [accessed 26 October 2012]

and deep trance.

The mantra *am fuaim mara* or "I am the sound of the sea" is used to induce the *mysterium tremendum,* the experience of numinous awe as an eerie or horrifying, yet compelling, power.

The mantra *am dam secht ndirend* or "I am a stag of seven points" is used to gain the power of strength. This is what is known as a *buada* or "excellence" in Gaelic lore. *Buada* were traditionally given to heroes by goddesses such as Macha and Brighid. The later Gaelic charm known as the "Invocation of the Graces" is actually *Ora nam Buadh* or "Song of the Excellences" in the original Gaelic, and is sometimes represented as having been first spoken by Brighid. Cuchulain was supposed to have had more of these *buada* than anyone else.

The mantra *am séig i n-aill* or "I am a hawk on a cliff" gives the power of deftness, or (in the Carey translation) "agility."

The mantra *am dér gréne* or "I am a tear of the sun" gives the power of clearness, or (in the Carey translation) "purity."

The mantra *am cain lubai* or "I am the fairest of herbs" gives the power of beauty- other translations of this line render it as "I am the beautiful flower."

The mantra *am torc ar gail* or "I am a boar for valour" gives the power of courage, although it's an uncontrolled and savage kind of courage- Carey translates the same word as "harshness," others have "on the rampage." Brighid's boar the Torc Triath goes on a wild rampage through Wales in the Mabinogion (under his Welsh name of Twrch Trwyth).

The mantra *am he i llind* or "I am a salmon in a pool (i.e. the pools of knowledge)" gives the power of knowledge and wisdom. It's a reference to the Salmon of Wisdom in the Boyne river.

Carey's translation has "swiftness."

The mantra *am loch i mmaig* or "I am a lake on a plain" gives the power of great size or extent, although it isn't exactly clear what that means in practice.

The mantra *am bri danae* or "I am a hill of Poetry (and knowledge)" gives all the powers associated with poetry by the ancient Irish. Carey has "excellence of arts for beauty," but the reason for the different translation is that *bri* can mean either "a hilltop" or "a power" or "an exalted state"- it's the same root as the *brig* in Brighid. *Danae* is "the arts" in a broad sense, meaning all the arts of the *aes dana* or artistic classes. This mantra is especially suited for bardic practice.

The mantra *am gai i fodb feras feochtu* or "I am a battle-waging spear with trophies" gives the power of victory in battle, or as the gloss puts it "spoiling or hewing."

The mantra *am dé delbas do chind codnu* has been translated very differently by different people, but the version in Hull's *Poem-Book of the Gael* has "I am a god, who fashions smoke from magic fire for a head" while the gloss says the power of this line is "to slay therewith." So please don't try to use it on anyone.

In Hindu mantra practice, mantras don't yield up their *siddhis* or powers just by saying them once like the magic words in a fairy tale. Rather, they must be "charged" through thousands, tens of thousands or hundreds of thousands of repetitions, at which point the yogi reciting the mantra gains the *siddhi* associated with it.

I suggest that the "Song of Amergin" be interpreted in much the same way, as a set of mantras meant to provide specific *buada* after many, many focused repetitions in disciplined meditative practice. The first three could be repeated a few hundred times by a modern practitioner seeking to enter trance, or as a preliminary

to practicing one of the other mantras to gain a specific *buada*.
Just be careful which "excellence" you try for, because excellence in "spoiling and hewing" is likely to be of limited benefit for anyone trying to live a happy and healthy life in the modern world.
The mantras found in the "Song of Amergin," especially the first three in which the bard invokes the Sea realm, can be helpful in making practical use of the *Cauldron of Poesy* as a modern spiritual practice.

In the remainder of this book, I'm going to concentrate on the Cauldron text rather than the "Song of Amergin," but I'm going to interpret the Cauldron text through my understanding of Amergin's role in Irish mythology, including the other Amergin of "Does Greth Eat Curds". The underworld associations of both bards, and the strange pseudo-pregnancy of the second one, provide valuable clues to understanding the Cauldrons.

the three cauldrons text

Sometime in the 7th century of the common era, a few hundred years after Christianity came to Ireland but before the last of the druids disappeared into history, an Irish fili or poet-seer composed a strange text on the nature of his art, a text which has come to be known as the *Cauldron of Poesy*:

My fitting Cauldron of Incubation
Was given to me by the kindness of God,
it was derived from the mysteries of the elements.
A noble prerogative that ennobles a womb
Is the speech bursting out from him who has it.
I am gray-bearded white-kneed Amergin of the blue-tattooed leg
Performing my incubation in the three colors of poetry:
white and black and speckled verse.
Not alike does God send it to each person:
In some it is on its side, in some on its lips, in some on its back,
On its lips in the foolish, on its side in the talented,
and upright in the master poet.
Performing many horrifying displays, vast seas of poetry for Eber Donn.
Learning the laws of language
And the skills of my art,
This is the true purpose of my cauldron.

I proclaim the benevolent Cauldron of Wisdom.
It distributes the principles of every art,
It brings prosperity to every artist,
It magnifies every ordinary craftsman,
It builds up a person through the power of art.

Where is the origin of poetic art in a person; in the body or in the soul? According to some it is in the soul, for nothing is done by the body without the soul. According to others it is in the body, clinging to a person through the connection to the ancestors, but the truth of the matter is that the potential for wisdom and poetry is in every person's body, though it manifests in one person and not in another.

What then is the origin of poetic art and of all knowledge in general? That is not difficult to answer. Three cauldrons are generated inside each person who has wisdom- the Cauldron of Incubation, the Cauldron of Motion and the

Cauldron of Wisdom.

The Cauldron of Incubation is upright from the moment it is generated. It dispenses wisdom to people as they study in youth.

The Cauldron of Motion, however, magnifies a person after it is turned upright. It is on its side when first generated.

The Cauldron of Wisdom is upside-down when generated. If this cauldron can be turned, it distributes the wisdom of every art there is.

The Cauldron of Motion, then, is upside-down in ignorant people. It is on its side in mere practitioners of poetry, but it is upright in the master poets who are like great streams of wisdom. So it is that not everyone has the cauldron upright during the early years of practicing his art, for it must be turned upright by sorrow or joy.

How many forms of sorrow can turn the cauldron? That is not difficult to answer. There are four: longing for loved ones who are far away, grief at being separated from one's own people, heartbreak from loss of love and the holy sorrow of self-denial for God.

And there are two forms of joy that transform the Cauldron of Wisdom- divine joy and human joy.

Of human joy, there are four kinds: the compelling force of erotic yearning; the joy of health and freedom from anxiety, possession of the necessities of life as one begins one's studies; the joy of acquiring the principles of poetry and prophesy after long study, and joy at the coming of poetic ecstasy from the nine hazels of the Well of Wisdom in the otherworld, landing on the Boyne river as thick as a ram's fleece and flowing against the current faster than a racing horse at the midsummer fair once every seven years. When the beams of the sun strike the plants along the Boyne, it is then that the Imbas bubbles up on them. Whoever eats them then will acquire an art.

Divine joy, however, is the coming of holy grace into the Cauldron of Motion so that it turns upright, granting wisdom in both secular and sacred matters, the power of prophesy, and the ability to work wonders and give wise judgments. But it is from without that the joys come into the poet to turn the cauldron, although the joy is felt within.

As Néde mac Adnai said concerning this:

I proclaim the Cauldron of Motion:
Understanding grace,
Filling up with knowledge,
Dispensing Imbas.
A meeting-place of the waters of enlightenment,
Uniting the poet with wisdom.
A stream of prosperity,
Bringing glory to the humble.
A giver of eloquence,
And swift-flowing intellect.
It makes him mysterious,
A craftsman of chronicles.
It cherishes students
Who attend to its laws.
It establishes clear language
And moves onward to melody.
All lore is approached in it, and all lore given out from it.
It enriches the noble,
And ennobles the base.
It exalts reputations
Through praise poems
By law.
It distinguishes rankings
And estimates grades,
Grants the gift of good counsel,
Like streams of wise speech.
The noble brew in which is brewed
The Boyne's Imbas and all wisdom.
In accordance with principle,
It is reached after study.
It is quickened by Imbas
And turned upright by joy.
It is made manifest by sorrow.
It is the lasting power of Brig,
Whose protection does not fade.
I proclaim the Cauldron of Motion.

What is this Motion of which we speak? That is not difficult to answer. It is the artistic turning or moving or artistic journeying of the cauldron, conferring wisdom and honor and high status after it turns upright.

The Cauldron of Motion
Gives and is given

Confirms and is confirmed
Feeds and is fed
Magnifies and is magnified
Makes requests and also grants them
Proclaims and is proclaimed
Preserves others and is preserved
Arranges poems and has poems arranged
Supports others and is supported.

Good is the well of poetic principle,
Good is the cauldron of the fire of knowledge, in which speech dwells.
Good is the cauldron that gives all these things,
It has built up his strength.

It is better than the domain of any king
Or the inheritance of any commoner
Because it brings you to wisdom and kingly honor
Like an adventurer roving far from ignorance.

If you have any interest in Celtic spirituality or bardic traditions, you've probably heard of *The Cauldron of Poesy*, and you may well have read the widely-available translation by Erynn Rowan Laurie and her accompanying notes. You may have seen one of the several meditative exercises created by neodruidic practitioners or people interested in "Celtic shamanism," most of which follow Laurie's lead by interpreting the three cauldrons in the text as rough equivalents of the chakras (power centers in the subtle body) or the three gunas (qualities inherent in all phenomena) of Indian belief.

What you may not know is that there are other translations by academics in the field of Celtic Studies- Liam Breatnach and PL Henry- that they differ in various ways from the Laurie translation, and that it is by no means established that the text refers to anything mystical at all, never mind chakras, gunas or Celtic shamanism. So what's the truth of the matter? Is this the foundation-text of Gaelic mystical practice, or something much more mundane such as a metaphor for how education works?

The text known as *The Cauldron of Poesy* is found in a manuscript known to academics as TCD MS H.3.18. The core of the text seems to have been composed by a fili, a high-ranking professional poet, in the 7th century CE.[2] Ireland had not been Christian for very long at this point- if by "not very long" you mean a few hundreds years, which most people would consider long enough!

Whoever the author of the text was, he was definitely a Christian, which might come as a surprise. After all, the Laurie translation refers to "the gods" several times. As Laurie herself points out, though, the original text says "God." Based on the high status accorded in the text to such aspects of early Irish Christianity as exile for the sake of God, the author may have been not only a fili but a monk. This is not as outlandish a prospect as it may appear, as the fili and the monks were actually something like allies.

Fili were considered "nemed"- a word that originally meant "sacred" (as in a druidic worship site, or "nemeton") but in legal terms meant "privileged." A few druids still existed in Irish society when this text was written, but their status was much lower than that of the fili. According to the law tract called the *Bretha Crólige*, druids in this era were not of "nemed" status, but were legally equivalent to a low-ranked freeman of the tribe or "tuath." We know that they must originally have been of much higher status, so why did they rank so far below fili by the time the Cauldron text was composed?

Classical writers tell us that there were three sub-classes within what may be broadly considered the "druidic class" in ancient Celtic societies: the bards or poets, the vates or prophets, and the druids as such, of whom the druids were the highest ranked and most powerful. By the time the Cauldron text was composed, the

---

[2] 'Cauldron of Poesy'
<http://www.obsidianmagazine.com/Pages/cauldronpoesy.html> [accessed 4 November 2012]

situation in Ireland was quite different- the poets were divided into multiple ranks of which only the lower levels were referred to as "bards" while the higher levels were called "fili," and the druids were seen as mere magicians of much lower status than the fili.

However, one synonym for "fili" was "fáith" or "prophet." This is the Gaelic equivalent of the word "vate," and may provide an answer to the question. It seems that those druids who were unwilling to accommodate themselves to the new religion suffered a loss of status, dwindled into low-payed magicians and then eventually disappeared.

The vates or prophets, on the other hand, seem to have survived the transition to Christianity by merging with the bards, adopting the new religion, and becoming the fili. So closely did the fili identify themselves with the church that they modeled their highly structured organizational hierarchy on that of the church. They also developed a new system of poetic meters called *dan direach* or "difficult verse" that was very much more complicated than anything used by the bards in pagan Ireland, and could only be used successfully after years of study. By adopting Christianity, merging with the bards, and developing an elite art form that brought both status and wealth to those who could practice it, the vates not only survived the conversion but became one of the most powerful classes in medieval Ireland. For the vates who became the fili, the coming of Christianity to Ireland was the opportunity for a power play.

It is very possible that some of these early fili were not only vates but druids proper- those who could see which way the wind was blowing. If you've ever wondered why Ireland converted so easily to Christianity- a nearly bloodless process, unlike in many other countries- just consider the constant tension between the kings and the Brahmins in early India. To an ancient Irish tribal king, converting to Christianity and ordering his people to do the same was probably the easiest way to get rid of his biggest rivals for real power within the tribe- the druids. Imagine the same king's irritation when some of those druids changed their spots and became "fili" with the blessing of the Church. By adapting to circumstances and becoming Christian, elements of the druidic intelligentsia were able to preserve, maintain and eventually even expand their power in Irish society.

So, the author of our text was a Christian fili, but his profession preserved lore and traditions going back to the pre-Christian era. As the centuries went by, the fili dropped more and more of the "druidic" elements of their profession and concentrated more and more on their status as elite poets with the power to praise or satirize the ruling chiefs. Sometime in the 11th century, a second fili wrote a series of glosses on the original Cauldron text, to clarify the meaning of some of its obscure phrases. Even though the glosses were written centuries after the original text, they most likely preserve an ongoing oral tradition of interpretation and commentary relating to the professional training of the bardic guild- the class of professional poets, including both the lower-ranked bards and the higher-ranked fili. (The glosses sometimes use the word "bard" loosely to refer to both, just as we do today.)

Around the year 1500, the Cauldron text and its accompanying glosses were copied over into the manuscript known to scholars as TCD MS H.3.18. A transcription of this text was included by scholar Annie Powers in *Anecdota from Irish Manuscripts* in 1913, and then Liam Breatnach organized the material, tried to correct some apparently corrupted word-forms in it, and published his translation in Volume 32 of an academic journal called *Eriu* in 1981. PL Henry also did an academic translation, and finally Erynn Rowan Laurie did her pagan-themed translation in the 1990s.

Since then, interest in this text among modern pagans has been almost entirely based on the Laurie translation, including her interpretation of the three cauldrons as being something like chakras or gunas, and the widespread assumption that the text was both deeply pagan and in some sense "shamanic."

The only problem with this is that Laurie's translation differs from the academic translations at several points, and the differences have a big impact on how "shamanic" the text seems to be. For instance, where Laurie has "for Eber and Donn,/ the making of fearful poetry,/ vast, mighty draughts of death-spells," Breatnach has "in order to compose poetry for Eber and Donn with many great chantings". This is not a minor difference!

The differences in translation are matched by equally huge differences in interpretation. To Laurie, the Cauldron text is essentially yogic- the outline of a spiritual or meditative system. To Breatnach, the text is simply an elaborate metaphor for the fili's educational process, using the cauldrons as a mental symbol for the process of internalizing and digesting both technical skill in poetry and the emotions used to inspire it. To Laurie, there are three cauldrons located in the belly, chest and head respectively. To Breatnach, there is only one cauldron with three different names depending on the poet's level of relative skill and training, and it doesn't exist at all except as a concept.

In addition, Laurie does not include the medieval glosses, which tell us how the fili actually interpreted the text. Breatnach does. Finally, Laurie methodically removes Christian references in order to "paganize" the text, although she is perfectly up-front about having done so.

As a practicing pagan with a deep interest in mysticism, I wanted to work with the Cauldrons text but was uncertain I could rely on the Laurie translation. I wanted to know what the glosses said, and why some of the lines in Laurie's translation were so different from Breatnach's. The only way I could know for sure was to delve into the original text myself, so I acquired a copy of the

Breatnach translation (which includes the original Old Irish) and got to work.

I used the Breatnach article to get the glosses (which are not widely available, yet substantially impact the interpretation) and for clarification on a few very obscure words found only in this one text. Then I used my knowledge of modern Gaelic as a guide, as I researched every word I could find individually in the Old Irish text to see what any Old Irish dictionaries (eDiL and others) or any other online academic sources said about that particular word, its meanings and associations. Finally, I tried to express each line so as to incorporate as many layers as possible of the interpretation suggested by the glosses (in some cases, actually adding lines from the glosses) or implications suggested by the historical usage of the word. For instance, one word was translated as "knowledge" by Breatnach, but was apparently used by ancient Irish writers as a synonym for Latin "sapientia" which is specifically spiritual knowledge or enlightenment- so I translated it as "enlightenment."

In the process of analyzing and translating this text word-for-word, I came to certain conclusions. The differences between Laurie's version and the others are so great that those familiar with the Breatnach and Henry translations have been known to tell interested pagans to avoid the Laurie translation and seek out the academic versions if they want to know what the text "actually says." Having gone over it word by word and line by line, I don't believe this is a fair assessment.

In lines where the Laurie translation differs greatly from the Breatnach, there is usually something in the connotations of the original Old Irish word or in the implications of the gloss that Laurie seems to have been trying to express with her interpretation. Breatnach was generally more cautious, and stuck to the denotation or "plain sense" of the original word. For instance, where Breatnach has "is the fine speech which pours forth from it," Laurie gives us "that pours forth a terrifying stream of speech from the mouth." The Laurie version is certainly more dramatic, and the cynical interpretation would be that this is because she didn't translate the original faithfully in order to make it sound more "druidic." When we look at the Old Irish, we find that the crucial word here is "brúchtas."

According to the Electronic Dictionary of the Irish language, the word "brúcht" means "a burst, bursting, breaking out; pouring out." It is used in phrases referring to water bursting out from broken dykes or erupting violently.[3]

So, although Breatnach is perfectly correct to translate it as "pours forth," the word in Old Irish has clear connotations of waters erupting from the earth or pouring forth in a dangerous torrent. So Laurie is equally correct to translate the word as "pours forth a terrifying stream." She was simply trying to incorporate more of the layers of implication in the original word, while Breatnach restricted himself to the basic meaning. Both translations are "what it actually says" unless we believe that only denotations matter and connotations do not. To a trained Irish fili of the era when the text was composed, the word and its associated images would probably have evoked a mental picture of the Well of Segais when it burst out against the goddess Boann- especially since the Well of Segais is functionally equivalent to one of the three cauldrons in the text, which even refers to a cauldron as a well.

In the very few cases where I could find no reason for the translation as given by Laurie, I assume the same explanation still

---

[3] 'eDIL Electronic Dictionary of the Irish Language' <http://www.dil.ie/results-list.asp?Fuzzy=0&cv=1&searchtext=(id%20contains%20B)%20and%20(column%20contains%20209)&sortField=ID&sortDIR=65602&respage=0&resperpage=10&bhcp=1&TOSSED=BACK> [accessed 4 November 2012]

holds but that I just couldn't see what her reasoning was. However, in my own translation I incorporated only the plain sense of the word or the connotations I could personally confirm or the information given in the glosses. Because my version of the text incorporates material from the glosses, it is more of a paraphrase than a straight translation. However, there is nothing in my version that cannot be found in either the text or its glosses, so it is a faithful record of the text's traditional meaning to the medieval fili.

My other conclusion is that not only are both translations correct, both interpretations are as well. When you examine the text very closely, it becomes quite clear that it is a metaphor for the process of poetic training and education just as Breatnach suggests; it also becomes quite clear that it is a yogic text just as Laurie suggests. The text refers to three cauldrons just as Laurie says, but uses ambiguous language implying that the three cauldrons are really just one cauldron, as Breatnach says. The text was written by a Christian fili, as the Breatnach translation would have it, but the fili was describing a tradition with clearly pre-Christian roots, as Laurie would have it. Neither one of them is wrong, they just chose to emphasize different things.

In the process of analyzing the text so closely in order to find out what it really said for myself, I realized that the yogic system described by the text could be interpreted as having some similarity to concepts like the chakras and the gunas- but that it could probably be best interpreted on its own terms rather than bringing in outside concepts. For this reason, my approach to "Cauldron mysticism" differs considerably from Laurie's. Regardless of these differences, I want to emphasize that my research into the original text essentially vindicated Laurie's interpretation in my mind, and that I have the highest respect for her work and her research.

Despite the fact that I am personally a pagan, I kept the original text's mixture of religious concepts. As such, this version is most accurately described as "Celtic spirituality" in the sense of a form of spirituality that cannot be simplistically reduced to a pagan or Christian identity.

One final note. This is obviously not an academic translation, it's a paraphrase created specifically for the purpose of doing spiritual work with the text. I am not a Celtic scholar. If you are looking for an academic translation, consult the Breatnach or Henry versions. If you think either of these scholars is far more qualified to translate the text, you are absolutely correct!

comments on the translation

The Cauldron of Incubation:

*My fitting Cauldron of Incubation
Was given to me by the kindness of God,
it was derived from the mysteries of the elements.
A noble prerogative that ennobles a womb
Is the speech bursting out from him who has it.
I am gray-bearded white-kneed Amergin of the blue-tattooed leg
Performing my incubation in the three colors of poetry:
white and black and speckled verse.
Not alike does God send it to each person:
In some it is on its side, in some on its lips, in some on its back,
On its lips in the foolish, on its side in the talented,
and upright in the master poet.
Performing many horrifying displays, vast seas of poetry for Eber Donn.
Learning the laws of language
And the skills of my art,
This is the true purpose of my cauldron.*

Irish Text: Moí coire coir goiriath

"Coire" can mean either "a cauldron" or "a whirlpool," so there is a connotation of a spiraling power or force, like the spirals depicted on Irish neolithic stone carvings at Newgrange and elsewhere.[4] "Goiriath" can mean "warming" or "maintenance" (as in a son maintaining elderly parents) or "incubation" (in the sense

---

[4] 'Sanas Chormaic: Cormac's Glossary - Cormac (King of Cashel) - Google Books' <http://books.google.com/books?id=rX8NAAAAQAAJ&printsec=frontcover#v=onepage&q=Brigit&f=false> [accessed 23 October 2012]

of protecting an infant animal while it grows) or "inflammation" (in the medical sense).[5] However, even the meaning of "warming" can also refer to a hen warming (and thus incubating) her eggs.[6]

Irish Text: gor rond n-ír Día dam a dúile dnemrib;

"Gor" is "warm" (as in the Coire Goiriath) or "pious, dutiful."[7] Hilaire Wood on the Old Irish list archives reads "Ronír Día dam," as "which God has given me."[8] "A duile" is "from the elements/elemental." Instead of "dnemrib" Wood has "demrib" (the original transcription from the Old Irish), while Breatnach reads it as "ndemrib," meaning "mysteries."

The "duilean" or elements are mentioned frequently in Gaelic lore and folk prayers. In the article "Some Aspects of Celtic Spirituality," Sean O'Duinn suggests that the lore of the duilean is connected to the Hindu myth of Purusha. Some might consider

---

[5] 'LISTSERV 15.5 - OLD-IRISH-L Archives' <https://listserv.heanet.ie/cgi-bin/wa?A2=old-irish-l;ONLShg;200205061000580700> [accessed 23 October 2012]

[6] 'Studia Etymologica Indoeuropaea - L. Isebaert - Google Books' <http://books.google.com/books?id=igGuwCkH8VMC&pg=PA315&lpg=PA315&dq=ol+irish+%22gor%22&source=bl&ots=SJyG3qHwDh&sig=u3NqRlH1c0us1tg8P6YKjFCeeH0&hl=en&sa=X&ei=f_WGUJfzL-ifyAG75IDwCQ&ved=0CCkQ6AEwAQ#v=onepage&q=ol%20irish%20%22gor%22&f=false> [accessed 23 October 2012]

[7] 'JSTOR: Ériu, Vol. 47 (1996), Pp. 193-204' <http://www.jstor.org/discover/10.2307/30007444?uid=3739736&uid=2129&uid=2&uid=70&uid=4&uid=3739256&sid=21101301232131> [accessed 23 October 2012]

[8] <https://listserv.heanet.ie/cgi-bin/wa?A3=ind0209&L=OLD-IRISH-L&E=8bit&P=437540&B=--&T=text%2Fplain;%20charset=iso-8859-1> [accessed 23 October 2012]

this to be speculative, but in fact the connections are too strong for there to be any room for reasonable doubt.

In the *Rig Veda*, Purusha is the "Primordial Man." He is dismembered by the gods in the foundational sacrifice that creates the world:

> Purusha's head becomes the sky, his brain the clouds, his eyes the sun, his mind the moon, his flesh the earth, his hair the vegetation, his breath the wind, and his blood the water.[9]

Compare the following text on the duilean from medieval Ireland:

> It is worth knowing what Adam was made of, that is, of seven parts: the first part, of earth; the second part, of sea; the third part, of sun; the fourth part, of clouds; the fifth part, of wind; the sixth part, of stones; the seventh part, of the Holy Ghost... The part of the earth, this is the man's body; the part of the sea, this is the man's blood; the part of the sun, his face and his countenance; the part of the clouds, his thoughts; the part of the wind, his breath; the part of the stones, his bones; the part of the Holy Ghost, his soul.[10]

"Adam" is obviously how a medieval Christian would think of the "Primordial Man." O'Duinn further connects this concept to the statement in the *Seanchus Mor* that the druids claimed to be the creators of the world and the elements. Just like the Brahmins in India, the druids must have claimed that their sacrifices were responsible for continuously recreating and thus preserving the universe, by reenacting the dismemberment of the Primordial Man.

The Irish "Body of Adam" text specifically makes this into a microcosm/macrocosm concept, in which the duilean mirror both the parts of the body and the inner spiritual state of the individual:

---

9 'Monastic Interreligious Dialogue | Some Aspects of Celtic Spirituality' <http://monasticdialog.com/a.php?id=303> [accessed 29 October 2012]

10 'Monastic Interreligious Dialogue | Some Aspects of Celtic Spirituality' <http://monasticdialog.com/a.php?id=303> [accessed 29 October 2012]

The manuscript goes on to explain that if the earth element predominated in a man, he would be lazy; if the sea element prevailed, he would be changeable; if the sun prevailed, he would be beautiful and lively; if the clouds, he would be light and foolish; if the wind, strong; if the stones, hard; and if the Holy Spirit, full of the grace of Holy Scripture.[11]

So, what our text is telling us here is that the cauldron's power or essence derives from the same fundamental energies of which both the world and the self are made. Just like the duilean themselves, the cauldron is both within the individual person (in the physical body and in the psyche) and in the spiritual landscape of the divine realm.

Irish Text: dliucht sóir sóerna broinn

"Dliucht" is "prerogative" or due.[12] "Sóir" is "a free man," in other words one of the noble classes, or just a word meaning "noble" or "good."[13] Breatnach has "sóer sóeras," the second word of which means "ennobles."[14] "Broinn" is "belly" or "womb."[15]

———————

[11] 'Monastic Interreligious Dialogue | Some Aspects of Celtic Spirituality' <http://monasticdialog.com/a.php?id=303> [accessed 29 October 2012]

[12] 'A Checklist of Proto-Celtic Lexical Items' <http://www.scribd.com/doc/20623905/A-Checklist-of-Proto-Celtic-Lexical-Items> [accessed 23 October 2012]

[13] 'MacBain's Dictionary - Section 32' <http://www.ceantar.org/Dicts/MB2/mb32.html> [accessed 23 October 2012]

[14] 'eDIL Electronic Dictionary of the Irish Language' <http://www.dil.ie/results-list.asp?Fuzzy=0&scount=2&searchtext=fleid&sortField=ID&sortDIR=65602&resperpage=10&respage=3&TOSSED=BACK&bhcp=1> [accessed 23 October 2012]

[15] 'Focalóir Gaoidhilge-sax-bhéarla Or an Irish-English Dictionary. ... - John O'Brien - Google Books' <http://books.google.com/books?id=C30CAAAAQAAJ&pg=PA64&lpg=PA64&dq=old+irish+%22broinn

The gloss suggests that the location of the cauldron is not in the breast (as Breatnach has it) but the belly, and that the poetic speech that comes from the belly containing the cauldron is what is ennobling, probably to both the poet and the subject of the poem.

We know from the implications of the previous line that the cauldron's internal location has both physical and psychological components (like the duilean from which the cauldron is made). The area of the body that equates to the cauldron is the *broinn* or "belly/womb." This is equivalent to what the Japanese would call the *hara* or what Taoists would call the "lower *dantien*"- traditionally a spiritual center of the body in Asian belief, and pictured by Taoist alchemists as a cauldron.

The core idea of this line is that the ability to declaim poetry from the center of your body has an ennobling effect. It might seem counter-intuitive to translate the word *broinn* as "womb" when the medieval Irish professional poets were mostly male, but that is apparently how they thought of it themselves. According to an article by Amy Mulligan in the "Journal of English and Germanic Philology," the Irish poets frequently described themselves as being "pregnant" with poetry, or as creating their poems in a "womb of poetry."[16] According to Mulligan, Irish medical lore of the same era treated the uterus as a "cooking vessel" like a

---

%22&source=bl&ots=zhrOB_iKiu&sig=CD3W4w6oNg2gkGb7--Pn6R9mfb8&hl=en&sa=X&ei=iieHUKy5L4XnyAH1toHACA&ved=0CFEQ6AEwBg#v=onepage&q=old%20irish%20%22broinn%22&f=false> [accessed 23 October 2012]

16 'Project MUSE - "The Satire of the Poet Is a Pregnancy": Pregnant Poets, Body Metaphors, and Cultural Production in Medieval Ireland' <http://muse.jhu.edu/login?auth=0&type=summary&url=/journals/journal_of_english_and_germanic_philology/v108/108.4.mulligan.html> [accessed 23 October 2012]

cauldron.

Mulligan references the legend of the second Amergin, the son of Ecet Salach. This Amergin was originally a mute boy with a hugely swollen (in other words, "pregnant") belly. The boy's fugue state seems to imply that he was mentally absent from our world because he was present in the otherworld. In any case, when he suddenly "snaps out of it" as a teenage boy, he quickly becomes a master poet.

This legend is directly related to the concept of incubation and the Cauldron text. But why did the Irish poets imagine themselves as being (in some sense) pregnant women? Medieval Irish law codes also treat the relationship between the tribal king and his chief poet as being like a marriage, and one source even states that the poet had a legal right to share the king's bed. The idea in this case is that the poet in his professional role as a dispenser of either praise poetry or satire is a stand-in for the territorial Sovereignty goddess who either grants or withdraws her favor to her mortal husband, the tribal king.

One of the duties and privileges of the poet, mentioned both in the Cauldron text and other sources, was to prophesy through Imbas or the mystical power of inspiration. The word "fáith" or "prophet" (from the Celtic "vate") is even used as a synonym for "fili" or professional poet in some texts. Yet legendary references to prophesy through Imbas usually portray the prophet as either a woman (like Fedelm in the Ulster Cycle) or a goddess (like the Morrigan after the Second Battle of Moytura).

We know that the Irish poets worshiped the goddess Brighid as their protector and source of inspiration, but the evidence suggests they actually saw themselves as incarnations of the power of the goddess in human form, mimicking her functions of prophesy, granting or withholding the blessing of the land to the tribal king, and "incubating" poetry and oracular wisdom in their "wombs."

The legendary references to female prophets like Fedelm may indicate that the role of professional poet was frequently taken by women in pre-Christian times, but in the medieval era women poets were only grudgingly tolerated by their male counterparts. One Scottish Gaelic poem even includes the line "I hate a poet-band that includes a woman," in a long list of things the extraordinarily cantankerous bard apparently hates.

It may even be the case that the role of prophet and stand-in for the goddess was originally exclusively open to women, and that male poets could only claim it by adopting a feminine persona-from which they eventually succeeded in nearly driving women out of the profession completely. However, there's also another way to look at it. One of the basic ideas of many forms of mysticism is the identity of the individual human spirit with the divine. By imagining themselves as *being* the goddess rather than simply worshiping her from afar, the Irish poets embodied a concept that many great mystics have described as the core spiritual truth for human beings: "thou art that."

So, this line of the Cauldron text contains rich implications for spiritual practice. Laurie's interpretation of the three cauldrons as being equivalent to chakras is not explicitly supported in the text for the most part, but her association of the Cauldron of Incubation with a spiritual center located in the belly absolutely is. There may be a closer parallel with the Taoist *dantien* concept, because there are supposed to be three of these *dantien* of which the lowest one is located in the belly.

Irish Text: bélrae mbil brúchtas úad.

"Bélrae" is "speech" or "language."[17] "Mbil" is actually "beil" in

---

17'(164) - Early Gaelic Book Collections > Matheson Collection > Old-Irish Paradigms and Selections from the Old-Irish Glosses - Digital Archive - National Library of Scotland' <http://digital.nls.uk/early-gaelic-book-collections/pageturner.cfm?id=80951527&mode=transcription> [accessed 23 the original transcription. Breatnach says it could be a corrupted form of "bél," or "lip," but reads it as an adjective "bil." "Brúchtas" is "pouring out" or "bursting out" as in a river bursting up from a spring.[18] "Uad" is "from him."[19]

The text implies that cultivation of breath control for poetic recitation (and mental centering) is part of the initial training associated with the Coire Goiriath or Cauldron of Incubation, because speech could only "burst out" of your belly in this way if you trained in breath techniques to project your voice from your abdomen the way professional singers do.

The use of a word normally used to describe water bursting up or gushing out from a spring also implies a connection to the legends of the goddess who causes the Well of Wisdom to overflow. This goddess is always named after whichever local river she is associated with, so in the vicinity of the River Shannon the goddess is called Sinend while in reference to the River Boyne she is called Boann.

The glosses to the Cauldron text make several references to the rivers Boann and Graney as the sources of the Imbas. This is particularly significant for two reasons. One is that the Well of Segais or Well of Wisdom is equivalent to the Cauldron of Wisdom in this text. (A later line in the text even refers to the cauldron as a well.)

―――――――

October 2012]

18 'eDIL Electronic Dictionary of the Irish Language' <http://www.dil.ie/results-list.asp?Fuzzy=0&cv=1&searchtext=(id%20contains%20B)%20and%20(column%20contains%20209)&sortField=ID&sortDIR=65602&respage=0&resperpage=10&bhcp=1> [accessed 23 October 2012]

19 'LISTSERV 15.5 - OLD-IRISH-L Archives' <https://listserv.heanet.ie/cgi-bin/wa?A2=old-irish-l;NLh5HA;200203071121460800> [accessed 23 October 2012]

Another is that Brighid, the goddess of the poets, is described in "Cormac's Glossary" as the daughter of the Dagda. Some legends describe the god Aengus as being Brighid's brother.

In the legend of the overflowing well, the goddess Boann is the wife of a god named Necthainn who is the keeper of the Well of Segais in the otherworld. Nine hazel trees surround the well, and salmons eat the hazel nuts that drop in the water. Only Nechtainn and his cupbearers may approach the well, so it is taboo for Boann. The Dagda- a god of druidic knowledge and much else besides- has an affair with Boann, who becomes pregnant. The Dagda stops the sun in the sky for nine months so her husband won't notice her pregnancy, and she gives birth to Aengus who is then hidden away in the Sidhe or otherworld realm of Midir. (It seems plausible that Brighid was also supposed to have been born at this time, making Aengus her fraternal twin, but the story as it has come down to us does not say this.)

According to the *Metrical Dindsenchas*, Boann is distraught by all these events and goes to the Well of Segais either to purify herself or to defy her husband's monopoly on the source of wisdom. The waters of the Well rise up against her and she flees toward the ocean, but she is dismembered by the rising flood (like a female Purusha) and carried by the gushing waters into the mortal world as the River Boyne. The same text makes it clear that the Boyne was essentially the Irish equivalent of the holy Ganges, because it is described as being somehow the source of every major river on Earth- including the Tigris and the Euphrates, the ancient cradles of human civilization. So this is not merely a legend in which a goddess is punished for violating a taboo- in fact, Boann's action is one of self-sacrifice, making it possible for the sacred waters of wisdom to flow from the otherworld to the mortal realm.

Boann's (possible) daughter Brighid is a goddess of flame and the dawn and the light of the sun, moon and stars- one Gaelic prayer says she "put beam on moon and sun." Boann is an Irish version of the widespread Celtic river-mother goddess, one of whose many equivalents in ancient Gaul would have been Sequana, goddess of the source of the Seine.

The glosses to the Cauldron text repeatedly refer to the source of the Imbas as being either the Boyne river (and thus the goddess Boann who still lives within the waters, manifesting as the Salmon of Wisdom) or the Graney river (although Breatnach wasn't certain this gloss really referred to the Graney rather than to the sun, as the Gaelic words are similar) or to a beam of sunlight (in other words, the power of Brighid as a solar goddess) striking plants on the banks of the Boyne at midsummer.

As Boann the water goddess is the likely mother of Brighid the fiery goddess of inspiration (who is also associated with water and wells through the many healing wells named after her throughout the Irish and Scottish countryside), it may be that Boann and Brighid are in some sense two aspects of a single power- the mystical combination of water and fire, which was of great significance in Celtic religion. For instance, the Romano-British goddess Sulis-Minerva was a healing deity associated with both a sacred spring and the power of the sun.

The Cauldron glosses describe the Imbas as arising from the power of water (the Boyne river which "burst out" from the Well of Wisdom) and the power of fire (as beams of sunlight in one gloss and as the "fire of knowledge" in another). Thus, the use of the word "brúchtas" or "burst out" is not incidental. Poetic speech "bursts out" from the poet who possesses the Cauldron just as the Well of Segais burst out to create the Boyne.

Irish Text: Os mé Amargen glúngel garrglas gréliath

Comments: Glúngel is "white-knee."[20] Breatnach translates "garrglas" as "blue-shanked," and the gloss actually says that this refers to tattooing. Gréliath is "gray-haired" or "gray-bearded" if "gré" is read as "greann" as Breatnach also suggests.[21]

Irish Text: gním mo goriath crothaib condelgib indethar dath

"Gním" is "doing" or "performing" or "making."[22] "Crothaib condelib Indeithear dath" is "with appropriate forms/ (in which) colour is made known" in the Henry translation.

The gloss specifies that the three colors of poetry are black, white and speckled. This is a reference to the three colors of poetry or "dath an ai" in the *Bretha Nemed*: white for praise, black for satire, speckled (which is also the color of the poet's mantle and the color of the otherworld) for a poem of warning (which was more or less a form of extortion: "change your ways or I'll make a satire!").[23]

Irish Text: -- nád inonn airlethar Día do cach dóen,

Laurie has stated that she only translated this as "the Gods" because she is personally a polytheist; the original unquestionably

---

20 'Links to Pagan Ritual in Medieval Irish Literature'
<http://etudesirlandaises.revues.org/2697> [accessed 24 October 2012]
21 'MacBain's Dictionary - Section 21'
<http://www.ceantar.org/Dicts/MB2/mb21.html> [accessed 24 October 2012]
22 'eDIL Electronic Dictionary of the Irish Language'
<http://www.dil.ie/results-list.asp?Fuzzy=0&scount=2&searchtext=xmlid
%20contains%20gn%C3%ADm
%20&sortField=ID&sortDIR=65602&respage=0&resperpage=10&bhcp=1>
[accessed 24 October 2012]
23 'LISTSERV 15.5 - OLD-IRISH-L Archives' <https://listserv.heanet.ie/cgi-bin/wa?A2=ind0103&L=old-irish-l&D=1&P=8750&F=P> [accessed 24 October 2012]

says "God." "Nád" is "not."[24] "Inonn" is "alike."[25] "Airlethar" is translated as "send" in other texts, or "apportion/provide" in the Laurie and Breatnach translations.[26] "Do cach" is "to each." "Dóen" is "person."[27]

Irish Text: de thoíb, ís toíb, úas toíb --

Toib is "side."[28]

Irish Text: nemshós, lethshós, lánshós,

These three terms are all variations on "sofhis," meaning "knowledge" or "wisdom." The order is different from the previous line. The gloss makes it clear that the cauldron is upside-

---

[24] 'eDIL Electronic Dictionary of the Irish Language' <http://www.dil.ie/results-list.asp?Fuzzy=0&scount=2&searchtext=xmlid%20contains%20n%C3%A1d&sortField=ID&sortDIR=65602&respage=0&resperpage=10&bhcp=1> [accessed 24 October 2012]

[25] 'MacBain's Dictionary - Section 23' <http://www.ceantar.org/Dicts/MB2/mb23.html> [accessed 24 October 2012]

[26] 'The Old-Irish Verb [signed W.S. Without a Title-leaf]. - Whitley Stokes - Google Books' <http://books.google.com/books?id=fHkCAAAAQAAJ&pg=PA11&lpg=PA11&dq=old+irish+%22airlethar%22&source=bl&ots=o67fB4ejdt&sig=0WXSNXzMgCNHw900H2e9zAXvtiM&hl=en&sa=X&ei=_y6IUMPpBcO-yQGwoIGADQ&ved=0CDcQ6AEwBA#v=onepage&q=old%20irish%20%22airlethar%22&f=false> [accessed 24 October 2012]

[27] 'LISTSERV 15.5 - OLD-IRISH-L Archives' <https://listserv.heanet.ie/cgi-bin/wa?A2=ind0712&L=old-irish-l&D=0&P=983&F=P> [accessed 24 October 2012]

[28] 'Old Irish Online: Master Glossary' <http://www.utexas.edu/cola/centers/lrc/eieol/iriol-MG-X.html> [accessed 24 October 2012]

down in the foolish, on its side for lower-level poets such as bards, and upright for master poets such as the *anroth*.

Irish Text: do h-Ébiur Dunn dénum do uath aidbsib ilib ollmarib;

This is one of the lines where the Laurie and Breatnach translations are completely different. Laurie has "for Eber and Donn,/ the making of fearful poetry,/ vast, mighty draughts of death-spells," while Breatnach has "in order to compose poetry for Eber and Donn with many great chantings." The gloss adds "with numerous displays out of the many 'great seas' of poetry".

"Dénum" is "making" or "performing."[29] "Uath" is "dread" or "horror".[30] "Aidbsib" is "great."[31] "Ilib" is "many."[32] "Ollmarib"

---

[29] 'eDIL Electronic Dictionary of the Irish Language' <http://www.dil.ie/results-list.asp?Fuzzy=0&scount=2&searchtext=xmlid %20contains%20d %C3%A9num&sortField=ID&sortDIR=65602&respage=0&resperpage=10&b hcp=1> [accessed 24 October 2012]

[30] 'MacBain's Dictionary - Section 40' <http://www.ceantar.org/Dicts/MB2/mb40.html> [accessed 24 October 2012]

[31] 'The Irish Liber Hymnorum - Catholic Church - Google Books' <http://books.google.com/books?id=tzieUzlI07UC&pg=PA277&lpg=PA277&dq=old+irish+%22aidbsib %22&source=bl&ots=CLGD5m7krq&sig=dJd39WG1kDI0ujCpeiA-Z6z59ys&hl=en&sa=X&ei=TzmIUO_RBpL3yAGBn4CQDA&ved=0CCIQ6 AEwAQ#v=onepage&q=old%20irish%20%22aidbsib%22&f=false> [accessed 24 October 2012]

[32] 'Sounds and Systems: Studies in Structure and Change : A Festschrift for Theo ... - Theo Vennemann - Google Books' <http://books.google.com/books?id=AK2MKUbzpncC&pg=PA209&lpg=PA209&dq=old+irish+%22many %22+ilib&source=bl&ots=bbT_LGXO_3&sig=tSmVSrIov9cbrr4p0FfyiavQRj E&hl=en&sa=X&ei=JjyIULX_CcKCyAHPhYCgDg&ved=0CB8Q6AEwAQ#

37

is "vast seas," as in the gloss referring to the poet chanting "great seas" of poetry.

Laurie has been criticized for making her version of this line so dramatic, but Breatnach seems to have disregarded "uath" or interpreted it differently. Both Laurie and Breatnach interpret the text to mean "Eber and Donn," but it actually says "Eber Donn."

Eber Donn was Amergin's brother. When he insulted Eriu, the Sovereignty of Ireland, he died and became the god of the dead and ancestor of the Gaelic Irish or "Milesian" noble families. The Milesian dead come to the House of Donn off Ireland's coast when they die. So Amergin is a poet performing for a king in this line, but also for the god of the dead.

This is significant given that the Welsh text *Preiddu Annwn* specifies that the Pen Annwn or "Head of Annwn" (Arawn, Welsh god of the dead) is the owner of the cauldron that Arthur and the bard Taliesin are trying to steal from the otherworld. The cauldron of wisdom from which Taliesin obtained his powers was owned by Cerridwen, the muse of the Welsh bards.

The reference to Eber Donn is also significant in the context of the earlier statement that God derived the Cauldron from the duilean. According to Cesiwir Serith's research into Indo-European comparative religion, Donn would most likely have been the Irish equivalent of the Primordial Man whose sacrificial dismemberment creates the universe. (An echo of this may be seen in the dismemberment of the divine bull named Donn in the Tain.) Therefore, the duilean of which the Cauldron is made could also be seen as the "Body of Donn."

**Irish Text: i moth, i toth, i tráeth,
i n-arnin, i forsail, i ndínin-díshail,**

---

v=onepage&q=old%20irish%20%22many%22%20ilib&f=false> [accessed 24 October 2012]

sliucht as-indethar altmod mo choiri.

These lines don't make much sense in literal translation because they have to do with learning the basics of grammar (masculine, feminine and neuter) and poetic skill (the length of vowels for rhymes) during the period of apprenticeship as a young poet. All translators agree that the last line means that this "basic learning" is the function of the Cauldron of Incubation, and the gloss confirms it (while adding some misogynistic comments about the masculine, feminine and neuter parts of speech in Irish).

The Cauldron of Wisdom:

I proclaim the benevolent Cauldron of Wisdom.
It distributes the principles of every art,
It brings prosperity to every artist,
It magnifies every ordinary craftsman,
It builds up a person through the power of art.

Irish Text: Ara-caun coire sofhis

"Ara-caun" is "I sing."[33] The gloss specifies that this is a cauldron of "good" (in other words, benevolent) wisdom.

Irish Text: sernar dliged cach dáno

"Sernar" is "it spreads."[34] "Dliged" is "law," which in context

---

[33] 'How to Kill a Dragon: Aspects of Indo-European Poetics - Calvert Watkins - Google Books' <http://books.google.com/books?id=Ri4sbTiMKN4C&pg=PA610&lpg=PA610&dq=old+irish+%22Ara-caun%22&source=bl&ots=GXt21EWO_H&sig=ungPByM6s72sPi2-W0DviK2oPOI&hl=en&sa=X&ei=wkiIULnWE-KbyQGgmYCIDQ&ved=0CCIQ6AEwAA#v=onepage&q=old%20irish%20%22Ara-caun%22&f=false> [accessed 24 October 2012]

[34] 'Contributions to Irish Lexicography - Kuno Meyer - Google Books'

seems to refer to the foundational principles of the arts.[35] "Cach dáno" is "each art." The gloss makes it clear that although the text refers to poetry, the cauldrons actually distribute the power for all forms of art. Therefore, practitioners of other art-forms can read this entire text as applying to their own arts as well.

Irish Text: dia moiget moín

Breatnach's notes indicate that his translation of this line is based on comparing it to other, similar lines in other texts. The idea is that the artist who possesses a skill is able to improve his material condition through it. This is due to the high status, income and honor-price of poets and other members of the *aes dana* or artistic class in ancient Irish society.

Irish Text: móras cach ceird coitchiunn

"Móras" means "magnifies."[36] "Cach ceird" is "each craftsman."[37] "Coitchiunn" is "ordinary" or "general" or "common."[38] The

---

<http://books.google.com/books?id=rxJgAAAAMAAJ&pg=PA482&lpg=PA482&dq=old+irish+%22sernaim%22&source=bl&ots=y_vOKtlaXC&sig=OfQ2WHLl1TKDdFzcdJ44-83LAgw&hl=en&sa=X&ei=c0uIUL2GB6HtygHdkYHYDw&ved=0CEIQ6AEwBA#v=onepage&q=old%20irish%20%22sernaim%22&f=false> [accessed 24 October 2012]

35 'Dliged - Wiktionary' <http://en.wiktionary.org/wiki/dliged> [accessed 24 October 2012]

36 'Old Irish Online: Lesson 7' <http://www.utexas.edu/cola/centers/lrc/eieol/iriol-7-X.html> [accessed 24 October 2012]

37 'Focal an Lae #240' <http://www.smo.uhi.ac.uk/gaeilge/donncha/focal/focal240.html> [accessed 24 October 2012]

38 'eDIL Electronic Dictionary of the Irish Language'

distinction between "dán" and "ceird" could be roughly compared to the modern distinction between "art" and "craft," so the text is telling us that even "mere craftsmen" can be ennobled by the power of the Cauldron.

Irish Text: con-utaing duine dán.

"Con-utaing" is "builds up."[39] "Duine" is "a person." "Dán" is "an art."

The Origin of Poetic Art:

Where is the origin of poetic art in a person; in the body or in the soul? According to some it is in the soul, for nothing is done by the body without the soul. According to others it is in the body, clinging to a person through the connection to the ancestors, but the truth of the matter is that the potential for wisdom and poetry is in every person's body, though it manifests in one person and not in another.

What then is the origin of poetic art and of all knowledge in general? That is not difficult to answer. Three cauldrons are generated inside each person who has wisdom- the Cauldron of Incubation, the Cauldron of Motion and the Cauldron of Wisdom.

Irish Text: Ciarm i tá bunadus ind airchetail i nduiniu; in i

---

<http://www.dil.ie/results-list.asp?Fuzzy=0&cv=1&searchtext=(id%20contains%20C)%20and%20(column%20contains%20319)&sortField=ID&sortDIR=65602&respage=0&resperpage=10&bhcp=1> [accessed 24 October 2012]

39'(168) - Early Gaelic Book Collections > Matheson Collection > Old-Irish Paradigms and Selections from the Old-Irish Glosses - Digital Archive - National Library of Scotland' <http://digital.nls.uk/early-gaelic-book-collections/pageturner.cfm?id=80951575&mode=transcription> [accessed 24 October 2012]

curp fa i n-anmain?

"Bunadus" is "body" but is used in compounds meaning "the bulk of" or "the origin of."[40] "Airchetail" is "a metrical composition," ie a poem, but is glossed as "poetic art".[41]

Irish Text: As-berat araili bid i nanmain ar ní dénai in corp ní cen anmain.

"As-berat" is "Say."[42] "Airali" is "other," as in "others say."[43]

---

40 'eDIL Electronic Dictionary of the Irish Language' <http://www.dil.ie/results-list.asp?Fuzzy=0&cv=1&searchtext=(id%20contains%20B)%20and%20(column%20contains%20244)&sortField=ID&sortDIR=65602&respage=0&resperpage=10&bhcp=1> [accessed 25 October 2012]

41 'eDIL Electronic Dictionary of the Irish Language' <http://www.dil.ie/results-list.asp?Fuzzy=1&scount=2&searchtext=xmlid%20contains%20aircetal&sortField=ID&sortDIR=65602&respage=0&resperpage=10&bhcp=1> [accessed 25 October 2012]

42 'Asbeir - Wiktionary' <http://en.wiktionary.org/wiki/asbeir> [accessed 25 October 2012]

43 'Ancient Laws of Ireland ...: Published Under Direction of the Commissioners ... - Ireland, John O'Donovan, Eugene O'Curry, William Neilson Hancock, Robert Atkinson, Thaddeus O'Mahony, Alexander George Richey, William Maunsell Hennessy - Google Books' <http://books.google.com/books?id=zcvUAAAAMAAJ&pg=PA71&lpg=PA71&dq=old+irish+%22araili%22&source=bl&ots=-ockm94rmP&sig=Vb5urDQuRr0sqfZ-JeDoidYDYWM&hl=en&sa=X&ei=cEyJUImOMoONyAGf2oG4DA&ved=0CCIQ6AEwAA#v=onepage&q=old%20irish%20%22araili%22&f=false> [accessed 25 October 2012]

Irish Text: As-berat araili bid i curp in tan dano fo-glen oc cundu chorpthai .i. ó athair nó shenathair, ol shodain as fíru ara-thá bunad ind airchetail & int shois i cach duiniu chorpthu, acht cach la duine adtuíthi and; alailiu atuídi.

"Fo-glen" is "adheres" or "clings to".[44] "Cundu" is "friendship" but Breatnach takes it to mean "relationship."[45] The text literally refers to "fathers and grandfathers" but this means "ancestors." The gloss refers to "inherited instincts" clinging to you through the body, making it clear that what the text is talking about is what we would now call a genetic predisposition or inherited talent. The text then goes on to assert that we all inherit the capacity for artistic creativity but only half of us can manifest it.

Irish Text: Caite didiu bunad ind archetail & cach sois olchenae?

"Didiu" is "then" in modern Irish. "Olchenae" is "the others," "the rest," or "in general."[46]

---

44 'eDIL Electronic Dictionary of the Irish Language' <http://www.dil.ie/results-list.asp?Fuzzy=1&scount=2&searchtext=xmlid%20contains%20fo-glen&sortField=ID&sortDIR=65602&respage=0&resperpage=10&bhcp=1> [accessed 25 October 2012]

45 'eDIL Electronic Dictionary of the Irish Language' <http://www.dil.ie/results-list.asp?Fuzzy=0&scount=2&searchtext=xmlid%20contains%20cundu&sortField=ID&sortDIR=65602&respage=0&resperpage=10&bhcp=1> [accessed 25 October 2012]

46 'eDIL Electronic Dictionary of the Irish Language' <http://www.dil.ie/results-list.asp?Fuzzy=1&scount=2&searchtext=xmlid%20contains%20olchenae&sortField=ID&sortDIR=65602&respage=0&resperpage=10&bhcp=1> [accessed 25 October 2012]

Irish Text: Ní ansae; gainitir tri coiri i cach duiniu .i. coire goriath & coire érmai & coire sois.

"Gainitir" is "born."[47] The gloss clarifies that the text doesn't really mean "every person," but only those whose "share of those cauldrons is generated." In other words, the general assumption that all people have the Cauldron of Incubation upright (and that only the other two need to be cultivated) is incorrect, because when the text says this cauldron is upright in "everyone" it only means "everyone in whom it is generated." Therefore, the first step in practicing this system is to "generate" the Cauldron of Incubation.

The Three Cauldrons:

The Cauldron of Incubation is upright from the moment it is generated. It dispenses wisdom to people as they study in youth.

The Cauldron of Motion, however, magnifies a person after it is turned upright. It is on its side when first generated.

The Cauldron of Wisdom is upside-down when generated. If this cauldron can be turned, it distributes the wisdom of every art there is.

Irish Text: Coire goiriath, is é-side gainethar fóen i nduiniu fo chétóir.

"Gainethar" is "born."[48] "Fo chétóir" is "immediately" in modern

---

[47] 'Indo-European Lexicon: PIE Etymon and IE Reflexes'
<http://www.utexas.edu/cola/centers/lrc/ielex/U/P0566.html> [accessed 25 October 2012]

[48] 'Indo-European Lexicon: PIE Etymon and IE Reflexes'
<http://www.utexas.edu/cola/centers/lrc/ielex/U/P0566.html> [accessed 25

Irish. The gloss says the Cauldron of Incubation is "a cauldron in which 'great falsehood' has been 'closed off.'" All three cauldrons must be cultivated in order, but in those with any potential for cultivation the first cauldron will always be generated in the upright position if it is generated at all.

Irish Text: Is as fo dálter soas do doínib i n-ógoítu.

The gloss clarifies that the cauldron distributes wisdom to people when they "enter into youth." Most likely this refers to receiving the basic bardic education, as this is implied by the poem about this cauldron in this text: "Learning the laws of language/ And the skills of my art,/ This is the true purpose of my cauldron." So when you are in the apprenticeship stage of learning an art, your study of the basic technical skills of the art "generates" the cauldron.

The cauldron inside you presumably "cooks" the information you've been given and then dispenses it to you. So this is a way of understanding the process of digesting, internalizing and being able to freely utilize the basic skills and knowledge of an art. Only once you have done this can you move on to the Cauldron of Motion. It seems likely that this cauldron is generated inside you every time you study a new art, skill, science or topic.

Irish Text: Coire érmai, immurgu, iarmo-bí impúd moigid; is é-side gainethar do thoib i nduiniu

"Immurgu" is "however."[49] "Iarmo-bi" is "after being."[50] Impúd is

---

October 2012]
49 'MacBain's Dictionary - Section 26'
<http://www.ceantar.org/Dicts/MB2/mb26.html> [accessed 25 October 2012]
50 'LISTSERV 15.5 - OLD-IRISH-L Archives' <https://listserv.heanet.ie/cgi-bin/wa?A2=old-irish-l;LMhxLg;200902171748040800> [accessed 25 October 2012]

"turn."[51] The gloss indicates that the cauldron is on its side when first generated, and that it "magnifies" the person after being turned upright. So, you must first generate the cauldron and then turn it upright.

Irish Text: Coire sois, is é-side gainethar fora béolu & is as fo-dáilter soes cach dáno olchenae cenmo-thá airchetal.

According to Breatnach, the words "besides poetic art" were apparently inserted into the original text at some later point, with a gloss clarifying that it means every other art besides "measured" poetic art. This makes sense, because a poet would already have the skill of composing measured poetic art long before activating the Cauldron of Wisdom, as this was his primary professional duty. The text without the insertion just reads: "of every art." I take this to mean that the complete activation of the Cauldron of Wisdom would provide you with the omnicompetence in all arts and skills such as is displayed by the Celtic heroes and gods.

Whoever has the Cauldron of Wisdom activated becomes an "Ildanach" like the god Lugh, expert in every field of human endeavor. This would be equivalent to the Asian concept that full enlightenment in one field can produce spontaneous mastery of all others, as in the case of famous swordsmen who were also great painters or calligraphers without additional training.

Considering that those who are described as having such a power in Celtic lore are all distinctly mythical figures rather than mere mortals, I consider it purely hypothetical for practical purposes- a mythic ideal to strive for rather than a condition to egotistically or delusionally claim to have achieved. Full activation of the Cauldron of Wisdom is a godlike state, and most can hope only to fully activate the Cauldron of Motion. This condition of becoming an Ildanach, possessing the skill of every art like one of the gods,

---

51 'MacBain's Dictionary - Section 23'
<http://www.ceantar.org/Dicts/MB2/mb23.html> [accessed 25 October 2012]

46

could be seen as the Celtic version of enlightenment.

Based on the legends of Taliesin and Finn, the source of the omnicompetence granted by this cauldron may be the full memory of all of one's past lives and the ability to access whatever was learned in each of those lives. (In Buddhist belief, the Buddha could remember all of his past lives- knowledge he most likely gained at the moment of enlightenment.) Taliesin tasted the three drops of Awen (the Welsh equivalent of the Irish Imbas, or poetic wisdom) from Cerridwen's cauldron of wisdom and he instantly became all-knowing. In his poems, he lists his past lives in many different forms:

I have been a tear in the air,
I have been the dullest of stars.
I have been a word among letters,
I have been a book in the origin.
I have been the light of lanterns,
A year and a half.
I have been a continuing bridge,
Over three score Abers.
I have been a course, I have been an eagle.
I have been a coracle in the seas:
I have been compliant in the banquet.
I have been a drop in a shower;
I have been a sword in the grasp of the hand
I have been a shield in battle.
I have been a string in a harp,
Disguised for nine years.
in water, in foam.
I have been sponge in the fire,
I have been wood in the covert.[52]

Finn, who tasted the three drops of Imbas from the Salmon of Knowledge on the Boyne river (whose otherworldly source, the Well of Segais,is equivalent to the cauldron of wisdom) later reincarnated as Mongan with full memory of his life as Finn:

---

[52]'The Battle of the Trees' <http://www.maryjones.us/ctexts/t08.html> [accessed 31 October 2012]

"I and the poet yonder," said Mongan, "have made a wager about the death of Fothad Airgdech. He said it was at Duffry in Leinster; I said that was false." The warrior said the poet was wrong.

"It shall be proved. We were with thee, with Finn," said the warrior.

"Hush!" said Mongan, "that is not fair."

"We were with Finn, then," said he.[53]

Finally, Amergin (the supposed author of the Cauldron text) lists his bardic powers in terms highly similar to Taliesin's list of past lives in the "Song of Amergin":

I am a wind on the sea
I am a wave of the ocean
I am the roar of the sea,
I am a powerful ox,
I am a hawk on a cliff,
I am a dewdrop in the sunshine,
I am a boar for valor,
I am a salmon in pools,
I am a lake in a plain,
I am the strength of art,
I am a spear with spoils that wages battle,
I am a man that shapes fire for a head.[54]

While Taliesin speaks in the past tense as if remembering past incarnations in many forms (including inanimate objects), Amergin speaks in the present tense. Mary Jones suggests that his could be a reference to the sense of unity with all things or *unio mystica,* a mark of spiritual enlightenment. The Cauldron of Wisdom, if fully activated, grants the highest possible levels of mystical insight.

---

53 'Tales of Mongan' <http://www.maryjones.us/ctexts/mongan.html> [accessed 31 October 2012]

54 'Awen' <http://www.maryjones.us/jce/awen.html> [accessed 31 October 2012]

Turning the Cauldrons:

The Cauldron of Motion, then, is upside-down in ignorant people. It is on its side in mere practitioners of poetry, but it is upright in the master poets who are like great streams of wisdom. So it is that not everyone has the cauldron upright during the early years of practicing his art, for it must be turned upright by sorrow or joy.

Irish Text: Coire érmai dano, cach la duine is fora béolu atá and .i. n-áes dois.

Based on the other glosses and text referring to this cauldron, it is clear that the author takes the position that approximately half of the human race has the capacity for some sort of artistic skill and creative talent, while the other half does not. Anyone can generate the Cauldron of Incubation in its upright position by studying an art or science, which will enable them to learn the basic skills. However, only about half of those people will have the talent to apply that art with creativity. For those without creative talent, their Cauldron of Motion is upside-down. They are not open or receptive to what is being poured onto the cauldron, so no matter how much is poured it will never turn upright.

Irish Text: Lethchlóen i n-áer bairdne & rand. Is fóen atá i n-ánshruithaib sofhis & airchetail.

Creative people are capable of generating the Cauldron of Motion, but it will initially appear on its side. In this position it is capable of being only partially filled. Artists of fair-to-middling skill and experience have the cauldron on its side, while masters of an art have their cauldrons upright. The references in the original text to bardic poets, composers of strophic verse and the "great streams" of poetry are all references to the strict hierarchical structure used by medieval Irish poets (the "great streams" were the highest ranks), but the basis of their ranking system was the poet's level of skill, experience and mastery of the poetic art.

Irish Text: Conid airi didiu ní dénai cach óeneret, di h-ág is fora béolu atá coire érmai and coinid n-impoí brón nó fáilte.

"Conid" is "So that it is."[55] Breatnach interprets "óeneret" as "at that same stage," meaning during the poet's student years.

The emotional experiences of life are not only the subject-matter of one's art, they are also what you pour into the cauldron to turn it upright. Just as the Cauldron of Incubation "cooked" the basic skills of the art as you internalized them, so the Cauldron of Motion "cooks" your emotional experiences as you transform them into artistic creations. You have to be open to emotional experiences such as joy and sorrow in order to generate the cauldron, but at first you are too emotionally inexperienced and thus too immature to do much with them.

However, as these experiences continue to pour down on your cauldron they eventually flip it upright. Now you can "cook" them to transform them into powerful art. This can be seen either in terms of life-stages or as something that happens over again every time you experience a powerful emotion.

Forms of Sorrow:

---

[55] 'Sengoídelc: Old Irish for Beginners - David Stifter - Google Books' <http://books.google.com/books?id=CqOZYQAx_xIC&pg=PA192&lpg=PA192&dq=Old+Irish+%22Conid%22&source=bl&ots=7FtAEiV6W-&sig=KchvXkMeUvLsMmxod4bCHswpSI4&hl=en&sa=X&ei=hbCJUMzMKcaiyAGvpYCgCQ&ved=0CE0Q6AEwBw#v=onepage&q=Old%20Irish%20%22Conid%22&f=false> [accessed 25 October 2012]

How many forms of sorrow can turn the cauldron? That is not difficult to answer. There are four: longing for loved ones who are far away, grief at being separated from one's own people, heartbreak from loss of love and the holy sorrow of self-denial for God.

Irish Text: Ceist, cis lir foldai fil forsin mbrón imid-suí? Ní ansae; a cethair: éolchaire, cumae & brón éoit & ailithre ar dia & is medón ata-tairberat inna cethair-se cíasu anechtair fo-fertar.

The glosses specify that the "longing" is for the poet's father. Obviously "longing" cannot always be so specific, but a young student in residence at a bardic school would most likely have missed his parents, so we can generalize this as "longing for loved ones who are far away."

The gloss specifies that the "grief" is for "people," which probably refers to the poet being separated from his own clan and tribe while at school.

The gloss states that the poet's jealousy is due to "cuckolding," which could refer to the fear that the girl the poet left behind may take up with another fellow while he is away at school. (Even though some of the fili were women even at this point in history, the text assumes the poet is male, as most of them were.) Thus, it is probably more accurate to think of it as heartbreak rather than mere jealousy.

Finally, the "exile for the sake of God" was a type of "white" or bloodless martyrdom practiced in the early Irish Church. It consisted of much more than just going on pilgrimage to holy places as Laurie translates it. The "white martyr" would go to some remote island or live alone as a hermit in the forest. There were other types of white martyrdom, such as vows of perpetual chastity[56], so again we can probably generalize this to include all forms of ascetic or self-denying religious practices. Note that there are three secular types of sorrow, and one sacred.

The types of sorrow and joy listed in these passages are the core of the entire system, as they make use of the historical meditation and composition methods of the Gaelic bards to achieve genuine spiritual insight through the transformation of your own emotions. Devotional or mystical equivalents of all these forms of sorrow could include longing for the deity, grief at the absence of the deity, heartbroken sorrow for the deity and ascetic practices in honor of the deity.

Forms of Joy:

And there are two forms of joy that transform the Cauldron of Wisdom- divine joy and human joy.

Of human joy, there are four kinds: the compelling force of erotic yearning; the joy of health and freedom from anxiety, possession of the necessities of life as one begins one's studies; the joy of acquiring the principles of poetry and prophesy after long study, and joy at the coming of poetic ecstasy from the nine hazels of the Well of Wisdom in the otherworld, landing on the Boyne river as thick as a ram's fleece and flowing against the current faster than a racing horse at the midsummer fair once every seven years. When the beams of the sun strike the plants along the Boyne, it is then that the Imbas bubbles up on them. Whoever eats them then will acquire an art.

Divine joy, however, is the coming of holy grace into the Cauldron of Motion so that it turns upright, granting wisdom in both secular and sacred matters, the power of prophesy, and the ability to work wonders and give wise judgments. But it is from

---

56 According to an article by Padraig P. O Neill in Eriu Volume 32- the same issue containing Breatnach's translation of the Cauldron text.

without that the joys come into the poet to turn the cauldron, although the joy is felt within.

Irish Text: Atáat dano dí fhodail for fíilte ó n-impoíther i coire sofhis, .i. fáilte déodea & fáilte dóendae.

Breatnach did not think of this text as referring to three cauldrons, but only one. Breatnach's cauldron starts out upright as the Cauldron of Incubation, is filled up with bardic learning, then emptied. It is then refilled with sorrows and joys to become the Cauldron of Wisdom. In between the two- as it is being tipped out and turned back upright- it is the Cauldron of Motion. This seems to me like a strained and artificial way to read the text, which definitely refers to three cauldrons.

However, the phrasing of the original text can be read as either "turns" or "turns into" depending on how it is read.[57] In addition, the text confusingly asserts that the Cauldron of Incubation can be either upside-down, on its side or upright (in the poem about this cauldron) and then that the Cauldron of Incubation is always generated in the upright position while the Cauldron of Motion is the one that can be in one of three positions. This logical contradiction can be resolved if we assume that there is only one cauldron at any one time: the Cauldron of Incubation (which is generated upright) becomes the Cauldron of Motion at the appropriate time (at which point it may be upside-down, on its side or upright) and can potentially become the Cauldron of Wisdom (at which point it is generated upside-down).

In any case, Breatnach reads this passage to mean that divine and human joy convert the Cauldron of Motion into the Cauldron of Wisdom, and Henry and Laurie read it to mean that these joys turn the Cauldron of Wisdom upright. Other passages in the text

---

[57] 'LISTSERV 15.5 - OLD-IRISH-L Archives' <https://listserv.heanet.ie/cgi-bin/wa?A2=old-irish-l;6cYxmQ;200911292122550800> [accessed 26 October 2012]

describe the Cauldron of Motion filling up with divine joy or grace and giving the poet the power of prophecy.

If the Cauldron of Wisdom is located above the Cauldron of Motion in an upside-down position, then the Cauldron of Motion will flip it over once it cooks enough of the divine grace. You can think of the text as referring to three cauldrons or to one cauldron; it doesn't affect the practice either way.

Irish Text: Ind fháilte dóendae, atáat cethéoir fodlai for suidi .i. luud éoit fuichechtae

"Luud" is a lever (or a battering ram), probably used to mean "a motivating force" or "a compelling force" that moves you as a lever would.[58] "Eoit" means "emulation" or "jealousy."[59] The gloss refers to cuckolding again- apparently something of an obsession of the glossator's- in a way that implies that the poet is driven to seek out sex due to his own jealousy at being sexually betrayed.

As this does not sound remotely joyful and also seems to be a bit of a personal issue for the glossator, we can probably set it aside except for one point- this is clearly not sex for the purpose of making babies, but erotic yearning. Since the text in general deals with the education of a poet, and the human joys all seem to

---

[58] 'eDIL Electronic Dictionary of the Irish Language' <http://www.dil.ie/results-list.asp?Fuzzy=0&scount=2&searchtext=xmlid%20contains%20fuichecht&sortField=ID&sortDIR=65602&respage=0&resperpage=10&bhcp=1> [accessed 26 October 2012]

[59] '(175) - Early Gaelic Book Collections > Matheson Collection > Old-Irish Paradigms and Selections from the Old-Irish Glosses - Digital Archive - National Library of Scotland' <http://digital.nls.uk/early-gaelic-book-collections/pageturner.cfm?id=80951659&mode=transcription> [accessed 26 October 2012]

correspond to specific stages in the poet's career, Breatnach interprets this to mean the "force of sexual longing" experienced in adolescence. If we accept this notion, the "emulation" in question might refer to the young poet emulating the sexual adventures of his peers or elders.

This is the "human joy" of sex for the sake of sex, the physical and emotional power of desire, the joy of Eros. In fact, the word in question ("fuichechtae") is often spelled "fuchacht" in other sources[60], which makes its real meaning crystal clear. This is a straightforward celebration of sexual pleasure.

The force of Eros is not only a major source of poetic inspiration throughout the history of literature, but a symbol of the supernatural sources of poetic inspiration. Great poets were believed to have fairy lovers or "leannan sidhe," semi-vampiric beings who granted poetic inspiration in exchange for some of the poet's life-force, often causing the poet to die young.

Irish Text: & fáilte sláne & nemimnedche, imbid bruit & biid co feca in duine for bairdni

The gloss on "nemimnedche" indicates that this joy has to do with freedom from anxiety. Breatnach reads it to mean that the poet has everything he needs in the way of food and clothing as he begins his studies.

Irish Text: & fáilte fri dliged n-écse iarna dagfhrithgnum

---

[60] 'eDIL Electronic Dictionary of the Irish Language'
<http://www.dil.ie/results-list.asp?Fuzzy=0&scount=2&searchtext=xmlid%20contains%20fuichecht&sortField=ID&sortDIR=65602&respage=0&resperpage=10&bhcp=1> [accessed 26 October 2012]

"Dliged" is "law."[61] "Ecse"or "éicse" is "learning" or "poetry," or "the profession of poetry" or "the bardic order," but can also mean the power of divination and prophesy possessed by poets. According to the *Colloquy of the Two Sages*, the power of éicse was activated by the proximity of water: "One day the lad went out to the edge of the sea, for the poets considered that beside water was always a place of revelation of 'éicse'."[62] "Dagfhrithgnum" is "good study."[63]

Irish Text: & fáilte fri tascor n-imbias do-fuaircet noí cuill cainmeso for Segais i sídaib, conda thochrathar méit motchnaí iar ndruimniu Bóinde frithroisc luaithiu euch aige i mmedón mís mithime dia secht mbliadnae beos.

This passage is densely packed with mythological references. One of the foundational myths of the bardic order was the story of the goddess Boann and the Well of Segais in the Sidhe or otherworld realm.

Breatnach was uncertain whether to translate one of the glosses on this passage as a reference to the river Graney or to the sun (*grian*). However, he translated the next line in the same gloss as a reference to beams of sunlight striking the plants along the

---

61 'Dliged - Wiktionary' <http://en.wiktionary.org/wiki/dliged> [accessed 26 October 2012]

62 <https://listserv.heanet.ie/cgi-bin/wa?A3=ind0012&L=GAELIC-L&E=8bit&P=7756&B=--&T=text%2Fplain;%20charset=iso-8859-1> [accessed 26 October 2012]

63 'How to Kill a Dragon: Aspects of Indo-European Poetics - Calvert Watkins - Google Books' <http://books.google.com/books?id=Ri4sbTiMKN4C&pg=PA75&lpg=PA75&dq=old+irish+%22frithgnum%22&source=bl&ots=GXt22LSP0N&sig=7L1Z09WbAlN2gvGMkrpBWLo_E2E&hl=en&sa=X&ei=sNGKUJLfBqnDyQHMyoCwCA&ved=0CB8Q6AEwAQ#v=onepage&q=old%20irish%20%22frithgnum%22&f=false> [accessed 26 October 2012]

banks of the Boyne river, causing bubbles of Imbas to form on them. Anyone who ate one of these bubbles would receive skill in an art.

This gloss is an example of a concept called "fire in water"- in Celtic lore, the combination of the principles of fire and water is sacred and magically potent. Beams of sunlight are usually described in Gaelic tradition as being the presence of a goddess- some traditions name Aine of Munster (whose holy day is midsummer, the day referred to in this passage), some name Brighid, who is supposed to have "put beam in moon and sun" according to one Gaelic poem. So the beams of sunlight from Aine or Brighid strikes the plants nourished by the water of the goddess Boann, and the Imbas bubbles up.

Irish Text: Fáilte déoldae, immurugu, tórumae ind raith déodai dochum in choiri érmai conid n-impoí fóen, conid de biit fáidi déodai & dóendai & tráchtairi raith & frithgnamo imale, conid íarum labrait inna labarthu raith & do-gniat inna firthu, condat fásaige & bretha a mbríathar, condat desimrecht do cach cobrai.

The glosses on this passage refer to some of the great wonder-working saints of the early Irish Church such as Colum Cille, who had the power of prophesy and of making true judgments about prophecy.

Irish Text: Acht is anechtair ata-tairberat inna hí-siu in coire cíasu medón fo-fertar.

According to Breatnach, the joys and sorrows work in opposite ways to turn the cauldrons. The sorrowful emotions are "produced from outside" the poet but they turn the cauldron internally, whereas the joys are "produced internally" but turn the cauldron from outside. The distinction between these two is not really clear. However, the gloss states that the "performing of their deeds"- prophesy and wonder-working- is what causes the cauldron to turn upright, which would indeed be a case of externally-produced joy.

The Cauldron of Motion:

As Néde mac Adnai said concerning this:

I proclaim the Cauldron of Motion:
Understanding grace,
Filling up with knowledge,
Dispensing Imbas.
A meeting-place of the waters of enlightenment,
Uniting the poet with wisdom.
A stream of prosperity,
Bringing glory to the humble.
A giver of eloquence,
And swift-flowing intellect.
It makes him mysterious,
A craftsman of chronicles.
It cherishes students
Who attend to its laws.
It establishes clear language
And moves onward to melody.
All lore is approached in it, and all lore given out from it.
It enriches the noble,
And ennobles the base.
It exalts reputations
Through praise poems
By law.
It distinguishes rankings
And estimates grades,
Grants the gift of good counsel,
Like streams of wise speech.
The noble brew in which is brewed
The Boyne's Imbas and all wisdom.

In accordance with principle,
It is reached after study.
It is quickened by Imbas
And turned upright by joy.
It is made manifest by sorrow.
It is the lasting power of Brig,
Whose protection does not fade.
I proclaim the Cauldron of Motion.

Irish Text: De sin, a n-as ber Néde mac Adnai: Ar-caun coire n-érmai

According to the gloss, the Cauldron of Motion sings to the poet, conveying "bountiful intellect" to him. The original text has a line attributing this verse to Néde mac Adnai. Breatnach includes this line and Laurie leaves it out.

Irish Text: intlechtaib raith rethaib sofhis

"Rethaib" could be "running" or (on the example of running water) "streaming,"[64] but both Laurie and Breatnach translate it as "accumulating."

srethaib imbais

I can't see the reasoning behind Laurie's translation of this line as " streaming poetic inspiration as milk from the breast," because "srethaib" just means "strewing" or "spreading out." She might have been trying to express some connotation or implication of which I am unaware.

Irish Text: indber n-ecnai

---

[64] 'LISTSERV 15.5 - OLD-IRISH-L Archives' <https://listserv.heanet.ie/cgi-bin/wa?A2=ind1112&L=OLD-IRISH-L&P=8634> [accessed 27 October 2012]

"Indber" is "a confluence of waters."[65] "Ecnae" is "wisdom," but was frequently used to translate Latin "sapientia," meaning spiritual wisdom or enlightenment.[66] Sapientia was also the Latin name for Divine Wisdom personified as a female figure also known as Sophia, who was the focus of much unorthodox mystical devotion and is still very important in the tradition known as Sophiology. Interestingly enough, Brighid has been referred to as a Celtic equivalent of Sophia or Sapientia in some recent sources. The best source for info on Sophia (including her role in Jewish, Catholic and Orthodox contexts) is probably *Sophia-Maria: A Holistic Vision of Creation*, by Thomas Schipflinger. There are no references to Brighid in "Sophia-Maria," but several writers have linked the two. For instance, Dennis O'Neill refers to Brighid as the "Northern Sophia" in Appendix A of his book *Passionate Holiness*. Eleanor Merry, in "The Flaming Door," wrote this:

> Bride, who is the soul of the ancient Mysteries - She is the Virgin-Sophia, the Virgin of Light whom the Bards once met among the stars.

And Alice Howell, in "The Dove in the Stone," wrote:

> There in the Gaelic tongue the prayers and songs rose and fell, with a Christian overlay, to the unflagging devotion to Sophia, first called Brith (or Brid), then St. Brigid, the Mary of the Gael....

Note that these are all recent Christian mystical interpretations, not ancient Gaelic lore. However, if "ecnai" in this text is being

---

[65] 'MacBain's Dictionary - Section 22'
<http://www.ceantar.org/Dicts/MB2/mb22.html> [accessed 27 October 2012]
[66] 'eDIL Electronic Dictionary of the Irish Language'
<http://www.dil.ie/results-list.asp?Fuzzy=0&scount=2&searchtext=xmlid%20contains%20ecna(e)%20&sortField=ID&sortDIR=65602&respage=0&resperpage=10&bhcp=1> [accessed 27 October 2012]

used as a translation of the concept of Sapientia/Sophia, the line could be read as "the meeting-place of the waters of Sophia," which would seem like a broadly similar concept to these recent interpretations.

Irish Text: ellach suíthi

"Ellach" is "joining" or "combining" or "uniting."[67] "Suithi" is "wise man" but "suithe" is "wisdom."[68] According to the gloss, the idea here is that the cauldron "adds wisdom to a person."

Irish Text: srúnaim n-ordan

The gloss indicates that this line refers to the cauldron's power to grant prosperity.

Irish Text: indocbáil dóer

"Indocbáil" is "glory."[69] "Dóer" refers to the lower ranks of ancient Irish society, the "unfree" classes. The gloss indicates that the cauldron raises up those of ignoble status by giving them an honor-price equal to those of noble origins once they achieve the rank of a professional poet.

Irish Text: domnad insce

---

[67] 'eDIL Electronic Dictionary of the Irish Language' <http://www.dil.ie/results-list.asp?Fuzzy=0&scount=2&searchtext=xmlid%20contains%20ellach&sortField=ID&sortDIR=65602&respage=0&resperpage=10&bhcp=1> [accessed 27 October 2012]

[68] 'Old Irish Online: Master Glossary' <http://www.utexas.edu/cola/centers/lrc/eieol/iriol-MG-X.html> [accessed 27 October 2012]

[69] 'Nach - Wiktionary' <http://en.wiktionary.org/wiki/nach> [accessed 28 October 2012]

intlecht ruirthech

"Intlecht" is "intellect." "Ruirthech" is "running swiftly."

Irish Text: rómnae roiscni

Henry has "reddening the eye," Laurie has "reddening satire," but both the gloss and the Breatnach translation refer to the "darkening of speech," the deliberately obscure *Berla na Filidh* or "poet's language." This was obscure, multi-layered and elusive language filled with archaic and pseudo-archaic words and phrases as well as poetic kennings that could only be understood by those with bardic training.

Irish Text: sáer comgni

The word "comgni" is used in compound phrases such as "comgni fer nÉreand" to mean "chronicles."
The gloss states the cauldron gives the poet knowledge of "the synchronism of kings".

Irish Text: cóemad felmac

A "felmac" is an apprentice bard.[70] The gloss says "It bestows cherishing on the students who attend to the law of the cauldron."

Irish Text: fégthar ndliged deligter cíalla

"Cialla" is "sensible" or "wise." The glosses refer to the students

---

[70] 'eDIL Electronic Dictionary of the Irish Language' <http://www.dil.ie/results-list.asp?Fuzzy=0&scount=2&searchtext=xmlid%20contains%20felmac&sortField=ID&sortDIR=65602&respage=0&resperpage=10&bhcp=1> [accessed 28 October 2012]

"attending to the principles" or the "laws" of the cauldron, and distinguishing the "senses of the language."

Irish Text: cengar sési

"Cengar" is "proceeds."[71] "Sési" is "melody."[72]

Irish Text: sílaigther sofhis

The gloss specifies that "many varieties of knowledge" are approached in the cauldron, and that he who has the cauldron then propagates that knowledge in his own students.

Irish Text: sonmigter soír
sóerthar nád shóer,

These lines talk about the power of the cauldron to make the rich richer (by providing a good living for hereditary poets) and to raise the ignoble to noble status (because poetic talent could raise you above your station in life in ancient Ireland). The old Irish legal codes clarify that a poet from outside the hereditary poetic

---

[71]'Italo-Celtic Origins and Prehistoric Development of the Irish Language - Frederik Herman Henri Kortlandt - Google Books'
<http://books.google.com/books?id=fyAbw-O31MoC&pg=PA97&lpg=PA97&dq=old+irish+%22cengar%22&source=bl&ots=8ZxgjJzB6r&sig=sjssW7C2cZomepL0R8a3Y7f9B_A&hl=en&sa=X&ei=i16NUK2zF8WcyQHmj4CYBQ&ved=0CGYQ6AEwCQ#v=onepage&q=old%20irish%20%22cengar%22&f=false> [accessed 28 October 2012]
[72]'eDIL Electronic Dictionary of the Irish Language'
<http://www.dil.ie/results-list.asp?Fuzzy=0&cv=1&searchtext=(id%20contains%20S)%20and%20(column%20contains%20154)&sortField=ID&sortDIR=65602&respage=0&resperpage=10&bhcp=1> [accessed 28 October 2012]

families could only claim reduced fees, but that if his children and grandchildren also showed poetic talent then his family would become a new hereditary poetic family with the full nobility and honors due to professional poets. So, even though it took three generations to reap the full benefits, poetic talent provided an avenue for social mobility. The glosses clarify- and repeatedly emphasize- that graduation from a bardic school provided legal immunity for the poet from the ill deeds of his low-class kinsmen!

Irish Text: ara-utgatar anmann
ad-fíadatar moltae
modaib dliged

These lines (and their glosses) refer to the poet's ability to exalt the reputations of those for whom he composes praise poetry, as long as all the proper laws and procedures are followed.

Irish Text: deligthib grád
glanmesaib soíre

The glosses on these lines seems to say that those who possess the cauldron gain the ability to correctly estimate the status and honor-price of others.

Irish Text: soinscib suad
srúamannaib suíthi,
sóernbrud i mberthar

These lines refer to the wisdom and power of the Cauldron as a drink or "brew." This directly parallels the concept that Sovereignty is a drink of some intoxicating beverage such as mead, served to the new king by the territorial goddess. Most likely, the bards pictured the Imbas as a brew presented to them by Brighid. The medieval Welsh prophets known as *awenyddion* described prophesy as a drink of honeyed milk. Due to Brighid's milk associations, the brew of the Cauldron may have been conceived of in the same way, but there are also numerous references to Brighid as a brewer of beer.

Irish Text: bunad cach sofhis

This line literally translates as "the origin of each knowledge (or wisdom)," but the gloss specifies that the Imbas of the Boyne river is what the line refers to.

Irish Text: sernar iar ndligiud
drengar iar frithgnum

The gloss says that the poet "climbs to good knowledge" via this cauldron after his bardic apprenticeship.

Irish Text: fo-nglúaisi imbas
inme-soí fáilte
faillsigther tri brón;

According to the gloss, the Cauldron is set into motion by the Imbas of the Boyne or Graney rivers (or possibly by the Boyne river and the sun). It is "turned" by joy and "revealed" through sorrow.

búan bríg
nád díbdai dín.

This line literally just says "it is a lasting or enduring power," but the word meaning "power" is "brig." This is the root word of the name "Brighid," the goddess of poets. According to "Cormac's Glossary":

Brigit i.e. a poetess, daughter of the Dagda. This is Brigit the female sage, or woman of wisdom, i.e. Brigit the goddess whom poets adored, because very great and very famous was her protecting care.

This matches our text, which refers to the protection granted by the Cauldron's power or "Brig." This root is also used as a prefix in a number of divine name compounds beginning with Brig. "Brig" may have been used in a very similar way to the Hindu word "shakti," which also literally means "power" or "energy" yet is simultaneously a word for the feminine divine power in any form. If so, this would explain Cormac's comment that any Irish goddess could be called "Brighid"- in Hinduism, any goddess can also be called Shakti. (However, not everyone agrees that Cormac's comment should be interpreted in this way.)

Analysis of the Cauldron of Motion:

What is this Motion of which we speak? That is not difficult to answer. It is the artistic turning or moving or artistic journeying of the cauldron, conferring wisdom and honor and high status after it turns upright.

The Cauldron of Motion
Gives and is given
Confirms and is confirmed
Feeds and is fed
Magnifies and is magnified
Makes requests and also grants them
Proclaims and is proclaimed
Preserves others and is preserved
Arranges poems and has poems arranged
Supports others and is supported.

Irish Text: Cid a n-ermae? Ni ansae: er-impud soi no iar-impud soi no eraim soi, i ernaid sofis s soiri s airmitin iarna impud.

Breatnach was uncertain that "soi" should be translated as "artistic" because this is a rare word in Old Irish. The glosses don't do much to clarify in this case. For instance, one gloss on this passage simply tells us that it is noble to turn knowledge toward some new purpose it has not been used for before. It goes on to reassure us that we will not be held liable for the crimes of our no-good kinsmen once we become professional poets.

Irish Text: Coire érmai,

The text just says "The Cauldron of Motion," but the gloss says "What is the analysis of Motion?". So, the purpose of this verse is to analyze the powers of the the Cauldron of Motion once activated. The glosses are essential to understanding this verse.

Irish Text: ernid ernair,

This refers to the fact that the poet gives praise (through his poetry) and receives gifts and payment from those he praises. So the Cauldron's power here is to allow the artist to produce successful work that will earn generous payment and material prosperity.

Irish Text: mrogaith mrogthair,

This line refers to the poet's role in upholding and passing down traditional lore. The poet confirms the stories and genealogies of other poets, and they return the favor by confirming his lore when he needs them to. The Cauldron has the power of making the artist a respected authority on matters of art.

Irish Text: bíathaid bíadtair,

This line refers to the poet "feeding" his hosts by entertaining them with tales and poetry, and being fed by them when they feast him and his retinue in gratitude. The Cauldron not only provides prosperity for the artist, but turns the artist into a person capable of providing prosperity to others. In this context, the Cauldron is like the Dagda's Un-Dry Cauldron that could never be emptied of food.

Irish Text: máraid márthair,

This line is about the poet's privilege of assessing the honor price of others in ancient Irish society, and the increase in the poet's own honor price as he rises through the ranks (eventually earning an honor price equivalent to a king's). A rough parallel in modern times might be the high social status associated with being a successful artist or a bestselling writer, and the cachet of being seen in such a person's company. So, the Cauldron grants the power of social climbing...

Irish Text: áilith áiltir,

This line is about the poet's ability to request special favors from the "tuath" or tribe, and the fact that the tribe also makes special requests of the poet such as to clarify difficult points of lore. So, the Cauldron grants the ability to ask special favors and have them granted by others. It also grants the status of one who is sought out for answers and advice, like a respected and successful author being asked to host a writing workshop or give a lecture.

Irish Text: ar-cain ar-canar,

The gloss on this line seems to be misplaced, as it refers to the poet's legal right in medieval Ireland to arrange pledges and sureties. This is more properly the subject of other lines in the same verse, as this line just says that the Cauldron "sings and is sung" or "proclaims and is proclaimed.". I would interpret this to mean that the Cauldron grants the power to create artistic work and be acclaimed by others for it.

Irish Text: fo-rig fo-regar,

This line refers to the role of the medieval Irish poet in ending clan feuds, tribal wars and personal vendettas through guaranteeing the peace agreement. The poet would pledge to satirize whichever party broke the truce. The poet also received almost total immunity from violence under Irish law. So, the Cauldron grants the ability to serve as a peacemaker through art.

Irish Text: con-serrn con-serrnar

The gloss on this line is obscure, but it refers to the poet's role in setting the standards for appropriate poetic meters- but the gloss says the poet can also expect to have the same meters used against him in the form of satires during litigation!

Irish Text: fo-sernn fo-sernnar.

The gloss says that this line refers to the ability of the poet to extend his safe-passage privileges to others.

We know from earlier sections of the text that the Cauldron of Motion "cooks" the emotions and life experiences of the artist and transforms them into beautiful and accomplished artistic work. Because the role of the poet in medieval Ireland still included oracular, prophetic and even mystical functions, these are among the powers granted by the Cauldron. However, this "analysis" of the Cauldron of Motion focuses on the material and social benefits to be gained by a successful and respected artist. The verse paints a picture of an artist whose work has brought material prosperity, the respect and acclaim of others, and high social status.

Realistically, all of these things are much less likely for a poet or artist in modern times than in ancient Ireland. However, if you achieve some form of external validation such as landing a book contract or selling a painting, you can take this as a sign that your Cauldron of Motion is active and working for you.

Concluding Verses:

Good is the well of poetic principle,
Good is the cauldron of the fire of knowledge, in which speech dwells.
Good is the cauldron that gives all these things,
It has built up his strength.

It is better than the domain of any king
Or the inheritance of any commoner
Because it brings you to wisdom and kingly honor
Like an adventurer roving far from ignorance.

Irish Text: Fó topar tomseo,

This line confirms the implied connection between wells of wisdom and cauldrons of wisdom in Celtic lore, because the cauldron is referred to as a "topar" or well. The line literally refers to a "well of measuring," but the gloss clarifies that it refers to the cauldron as a source of the basic principles of versification such as the verse-foot. Breatnach believed that this line referred to the Cauldron of Incubation, which would fit the rest of the text.

Irish Text: fó atrab n-insce,

The gloss tells us that the cauldron contains something called the *tein fesa* or "fire of knowledge." We have already been told that it contains a special "brew," or the Imbas of the Boyne river, so here we have another reference to the mystical power of "fire in water" in Celtic belief. Breatnach indicates that the phrase *tein fesa* in other texts refers to poetic inspiration, and says that this line probably refers to the Cauldron of Motion. Whether or not he's right that the Cauldron of Motion is specifically indicated here, this is a clear reference to one of the three fires of Brighid- commonly interpreted as the fire of the hearth, the fire of the forge, and the fire of poetic inspiration.

Irish Text: fó comair coimseo con-utaing firse.

Both Laurie and Breatnach have "good is the confluence of power which builds up strength," which Breatnach took to refer to the Cauldron of Wisdom. The gloss just says that the cauldron out of which all these things are obtained is a good cauldron.

**Is mó cach ferunn,
is ferr cach orbu,
berid co h-ecnae,**

These lines tell us that even a rich inheritance or a kingly domain would not be as good to have as a fully activated Cauldron, because the Cauldron brings you both high status and wisdom.

Irish Text: echtraid fri borbu.

Laurie takes "echtraid" to be the same word as that used for the great tales of otherworld journeys known as "echtrae" or "immramma," and "echtraid" itself does mean "adventurer" or "rover" or "wanderer."[73]

---

[73] 'eDIL Electronic Dictionary of the Irish Language' <http://www.dil.ie/results-list.asp?Fuzzy=0&scount=2&searchtext=xmlid%20contains%20echtraid&sortField=ID&sortDIR=65602&respage=0&resperpage=10&bhcp=1> [accessed 28 October 2012].

incubation

Now that we've gone through the Cauldron text line by line, let's examine how each of the Three Cauldrons works and what it does.

The name of the first cauldron is more significant than it appears, because "incubation" was one of the primary forms of oracular practice in the ancient world and is also known to have been a practice of the Gaelic bards. In temples all over the Greek and Roman world, worshipers seeking an oracle would sleep overnight (or for as many nights as necessary) at a temple or shrine. Part of the process of incubation is to sleep in total darkness, or even in an underground cave containing the shrine. The idea behind this type of incubation is that the worshiper is undergoing a symbolic descent into the cthonic realm, a death from which he will then be reborn with the gift of knowledge from the underworld.

This practice was known in Ireland at the time the Cauldron text was composed. Pilgrims would sleep at a cave known as St. Patrick's Purgatory in order to have visions of Hell, Purgatory and the dead. This cave might originally have been the site of a pagan incubation shrine such as those found elsewhere in ancient Europe. In any case the Church eventually closed the cave up to put a stop to the practice.[74]

The fact that Goiriath can be translated as "incubation" would present us with only the vaguest link to this oracular practice, if not for the context supplied by the text itself. Amergin tells us that he is singing for Eber Donn. Previous translators have read this as "Eber and Donn," and interpreted it to mean that the archetypal poet (Amergin) is performing for the archetypal Irish kings (Eber

---

[74] 'St. Patrick's Purgatory | Ireland Journey' <http://ireland-journey.com/news/st-patricks-purgatory> [accessed 26 October 2012]

and Donn of the Milesians). However, there is no "and" in the original text, which simply refers to "Eber Donn."

In Irish legend, Eber Donn was a Milesian chief and the brother of Amergin. When (unlike Amergin) he refused to show any respect to the goddess of the land, she cursed him to die without ever enjoying Ireland. When the Milesian warfleet was about to land, Eber Donn arrogantly proclaimed his intention to massacre every warrior he found in Ireland. Rejected by the land goddess, Eber Donn was now swallowed up the sea, which swamped his boat and drowned Eber Donn and his crew. After death, Eber Donn became the fairy king of Tech Duinn, the House of Donn. This House was believed to exist somewhere on or beneath Bull Island. The descendents of the Milesians were believed to go there when they died.

In other words, Eber Donn is the Irish god of the dead- and Amergin explicitly connects him with the Cauldron of Incubation. The myth of Eber Donn also parallels a statement of Caesar's to the effect that the Celts considered themselves to be descended from Dis Pater, the god of the dead. Eber Donn is the ancestor god of the Milesians or Gaelic Irish.[75]

Not only does Amergin tell us that he is displaying his art for Eber Donn, he also tells us that his performance consists of "many horrifying displays, vast seas of poetry." Eber Donn's death was caused by the sea, his House is beneath the sea or on an island in the sea, and the sea is one of the Three Realms of Celtic lore (land, sea and sky). In the Three Realms model of the cosmos, the sea represents the otherworld and the underworld as well as the actual sea. The chaos giants who fight the gods in the earliest cycle of Irish myth are the Fomorians or "those from beneath the sea."

---

75 As well as being a cautionary tale about the dangers of defying the land goddess and embracing mindless violence.

A close parallel may be seen in the Welsh poem known as the *Preiddu Annwm,* in which Amergin's Welsh equivalent Taliesin describes a raid on an underworld located either below or across the ocean to steal a magic cauldron from the god of the dead. Seen in this context, it is clear that the poem is a culture-hero myth in which Taliesin descends to the watery underworld and returns with the cauldron of poetic art.

So, if we look at all of the implications of the fact that Amergin is supposed to be performing for Eber Donn, we can see that the text connects the Cauldron of Incubation with the realm of the sea, the god of the dead and the power of the ancestors. Other sections of the text make direct references to the concept that the skill of poetry is inherited from the ancestors. Amergin also tells us that the Cauldron of Incubation's primary function or "true purpose" is to help the apprentice poet learn the laws of language and the skills of his art.

When we examine how apprentice poets actually studied these skills in the bardic schools of ancient Ireland, we find that they did so through a process strikingly similar to oracular incubation. The only surviving eyewitness account of such a school is the one found in the *Memoirs of the Marquis of Clanricarde,* given here as quoted by Bergin:

The poetical Seminary or School… was open only to such as were descended of Poets and reputed within their Tribes…

The Structure was a snug low Hut, and beds in it at convenient Distances, each with a small Apartment without much Furniture of any kind, save only a Table, some Seats, and a Conveniency for Cloaths to hang upon. No Windows to let in the Day, nor any Light at all us'd but that of Candles, and these brought in at a proper Season only…

The Professors (one or more as there was occasion) gave a Subject suitable to the Capacity of each Class, determining the number of Rhymes, and clearing what was to be chiefly observed therein as to Syllables, Quartans, Concord, Correspondence, Termination and Union, each of which were restrained by peculiar Rules. The said Subject (either one or more as aforesaid) having been given over Night, they worked it apart each by himself upon his own Bed, the whole next Day in the Dark, till at a certain Hour in the night, Lights being brought in, they committed it to writing. Being afterwards dress'd and come together in a large Room, where the Masters awaited, each Scholar gave in his Performance, which being corrected or approved of (according as it requir'd) either the same or fresh subjects were given against the next Day…[76]

At the apprenticeship stage in the poet's education, he works only on learning the techniques of his craft- he is not yet ready for the Imbas or oracular poetic ecstasy. Nevertheless, his method of study is to lie in complete darkness meditating on the topic at hand. In fact, the poet apparently never sees the daylight at all during his time at school, so that the entire period of his apprenticeship is effectively an incubation (punctuated by visits home and to neighboring lords to practice performing).

This description is confirmed by Martin Martin, a writer who described Gaelic culture in the Hebrides in 1703:

I must not omit to relate their way of Study, which is very singular. They shut their Doors and Windows for a day's time, and lie on their Backs, with a Stone upon their Belly, and Plaids about their heads, and their eyes being covered, they pump their Brains [for] Rhetorical Encomium or Pane-gerick ; and indeed they furnish such a Stile from this dark Cell, as is understood by very few, and if they purchase a couple of Horses as the Reward for their Meditation, they think they have done a great matter.[77]

This reference adds a crucial detail, because Amergin tells us that "A noble prerogative that ennobles a womb/ Is the speech bursting out from him who has it." The word I have translated as "womb" can literally mean either womb or belly. I chose to

---

[76] 'Bard School | Reginald Gibbons'
<http://reginaldgibbons.northwestern.edu/bard-school> [accessed 26 October 2012]

[77] 'Full Text of "Transactions"'
<http://www20.us.archive.org/stream/transactions29gaeluoft/transactions29gaeluoft_djvu.txt> [accessed 26 October 2012]

translate it as womb to emphasize some of the layers of implicit meaning:

1- that the cauldron, by granting the privileges of a professional poet to those of low social status, ennobles them and raises them above the status they were born with.
2- that a cauldron is often interpreted as being a symbolic womb.
3- that the process of oracular incubation is a symbolic death, time in the womb of the underworld, and rebirth.
4- that the medieval Irish poets (even though they were mostly male) sometimes described themselves as being pregnant with poetry, or as creating their poems in a "womb of poetry."[78] In other words, they visualized themselves as being the goddess.

Martin Martin's account of Scottish Gaelic bardic practice tells us several interesting things. One is that the incubation method was still used for all bardic composition even after the end of the poet's apprenticeship in the bardic school. Another is that the *broinn* (the"belly/womb") was considered central to this process. Another is that techniques of breath control were involved- putting a weight on the belly while lying down helps you to breathe deeply from the abdomen[79], a goal in many forms of meditation. This method of breath control was probably intended not only to facilitate the bard's meditation on his poetic topic, but to help him learn how to project his voice from the abdomen- as in the line in the Cauldron text stating that speech will "burst out" from the *broinn* of he who has the Cauldron of Incubation activated inside him.

Later, as a high-level poet qualified to practice oracular

---
[78] 'Project MUSE - "The Satire of the Poet Is a Pregnancy": Pregnant Poets, Body Metaphors, and Cultural Production in Medieval Ireland'
<http://muse.jhu.edu/journals/egp/summary/v108/108.4.mulligan.html> [accessed 26 October 2012]

[79] This is because, if you are breathing correctly from the belly, the weight will rise and fall with your breath.

techniques, the poet still uses the method of incubation (from *Cormac's Glossary* in the Stokes translation as quoted by Nora Chadwick):

> Imbas forosna, 'Manifestation that enlightens': (it) discovers what thing soever the poet likes and which he desires to reveal.(2) Thus then is that done. The poet chews a piece of the red flesh of a pig, or a dog, or a cat, and puts it then on a flagstone behind the door-valve, and chants an incantation over it, and offers it to idol gods, and calls them to him, and leaves them not on the morrow, and then chants over his two palms, and calls again idol gods to him, that his sleep may not be disturbed. Then he puts his two palms on his two cheeks and sleeps. And men are watching him that he may not turn over and that no one may disturb him. And then it is revealed to him that for which he was (engaged) till the end of a nómad (three days and nights), or two or three for the long or the short (time?) that he may judge himself (to be) at the offering. And therefore it is called Imm-bas, to wit, a palm (bas) on this side and a palm on that around his head. Patrick banished that and the Tenm láida 'illumination of song,' and declared that no one who shall do that shall belong to heaven or earth, for it is a denial of baptism.[80]

So, what have we learned here? That incubation was practiced as an oracular method by the Gaelic poets, that it was also their primary method of study during the years of apprenticeship, that it was associated with cthonic powers, the realm of the sea, the god of the dead, the knowledge of the underworld passed down from the ancestors, breath control techniques, and the region of the body known as the *broinn* or "belly/womb". This is how we should understand the Cauldron of Incubation, which is therefore much more important than generally assumed. The Cauldron of Incubation is the key to the method of meditation we will explore in this book.

There is another layer of implication to the concept of the poet's incubation. In the late Welsh story called the *Hanes Taliesin*

---

[80] 'Searching for Imbas: Imbas Forosnai by Nora K. Chadwick' <http://searchingforimbas.blogspot.com/p/imbas-forosnai-by-nora-k-chadwick.html> [accessed 26 October 2012]

(which is quite possibly based on Irish sources[81] combined with elements of older Welsh lore about the bard) Taliesin obtains the *awen*- the Welsh equivalent of Imbas- from the cauldron of wisdom, and is then chased by the witch Cerridwen (who may or may not have originally been a goddess) in various animal forms before she finally turns into a hen and swallows him in the form of a seed. She then gives birth to him nine months later and finally sets him adrift on the sea.

In ancient Ireland, the normal everyday usage of the word *goiriath* referred to a hen incubating an egg.[82] The *Hanes Taliesin* contains a cauldron of wisdom, an incubation in the womb of a goddess-like figure, a hen, and a reference to the sea. This tells us that the story is probably concerned with the same or a similar tradition as the Three Cauldrons text, having to do with the professional mysteries of the bardic guild.

It is therefore likely that the process of poetic incubation was conceived of as occurring within the womb of a goddess, which was simultaneously seen as the underworld and the realm of the ancestors. The Welsh bards called themselves "Sons of Cerridwen," while the Irish bards were devoted to the goddess Brighid. By the time this lore was put down in writing as the Three Cauldrons text, God alone is mentioned and no goddess appears. Given the date of the text, this is not surprising, but I believe the tradition would have originally specified that the incubation of the poet occurred within the womb of the goddess

---

81 Specifically, the legend of Finn and the Salmon of Wisdom.
82 'Studia Etymologica Indoeuropaea - L. Isebaert - Google Books' <http://books.google.com/books?id=igGuwCkH8VMC&pg=PA315&lpg=PA315&dq=ol+irish+%22gor%22&source=bl&ots=SJyG3qHwDh&sig=u3NqRlH1c0us1tg8P6YKjFCeeH0&hl=en&sa=X&ei=f_WGUJfzL-ifyAG75IDwCQ&ved=0CCkQ6AEwAQ#v=onepage&q=ol%20irish%20%22gor%22&f=false> [accessed 23 October 2012]

Brighid.

This implication is further supported by the fact that the term of study in the Irish bardic schools ran from the end of harvest until the beginning of spring. This is the same time of year in which Scottish Gaelic lore portrays Brighid as being a prisoner in the mountain fortress of the hag-goddess known as the Cailleach.[83] When spring began (traditionally on Brighid's festival day of Imbolc on February 1), Scottish families would celebrate by making a doll called the *brideog* or "Baby Brighid." The bardic study term ran a bit longer than this, lasting until the first cuckoos appeared, but the parallels are strong: Brighid is kept in a dark place all winter and then reborn as an infant, and the poet is in the dark cell all winter studying through incubation.

When we remember that the Irish poets spoke of themselves as being "pregnant with poetry," we get a kind of mirrors-within-mirrors effect here: the Cailleach incubates Brighid who incubates the poet who incubates the poem. The poet's incubation occurs within Brighid's womb, and the poet on graduating from his studies is the *brideog*; but it is equally valid from another perspective to say that the poet is Brighid and the poem is the *brideog*.

Taking all of these layers of lore and implication into account, we can say that the Cauldron of Incubation is the "dark cell" in which the poet studies; it is also the poet's own *broinn* or "womb of poetry"; and it is also the underworld. The Cauldron of Incubation is also the incubation method of study and meditation, a method used with increasingly deeper symbolic purpose as the poet matures in the poetic art:

---

[83] There is some question about the authenticity of the Scottish myth, as the maiden held captive by the Cailleach is not usually identified explicitly as Brighid in the oral tradition. However, Brighid's rebirth every spring strongly suggests that the identification of the two in some sources is in fact valid.

1- In the apprenticeship stage, the Cauldron incubates the basic knowledge and skills of the poetic art. At this stage, it is referred to as the *Coire Goiriath*.

2- In the journeyman stage, the Cauldron incubates the life experiences and emotions the poet needs to produce artistically mature work. At this stage, it is referred to as the *Coire Ermae*.

3- In the stage of mastery, the Cauldron incubates divine, mystical and ecstatic forces to transform the poet into an omnicompetent prophet, sage and magician like Amergin or Taliesin. At this final stage, it is referred to as the *Coire Sofhis.* Most people who actively seek this exalted state will only get fleeting glimpses of it. I don't expect to ever fully activate the Cauldron of Wisdom or to ever meet anyone who has. Instead, I think of it as an impossible ideal that we can improve our lives by striving toward.

The process of the Three Cauldrons system of bardic mysticism is a three-stage application of Incubation, beginning with the basics and moving on to the emotions before finally reaching out for glimpses of the highest levels of divine wisdom- and if you're very lucky, the three precious drops that will transform you into a "god who makes fire for a head"- a new Amergin.

motion

When comparing the Three Cauldrons system to other spiritual practices around the world, the first thing that stands out is that the attitude to human emotion is completely different. Consider this quote by the Greek philosopher Epictetus:

Remember that you must behave in life as at a dinner party. Is anything brought around to you? Put out your hand and take your share with moderation. Does it pass by you? Don't stop it. Is it not yet come? Don't stretch your desire towards it, but wait till it reaches you. Do this with regard to children, to a wife, to public posts, to riches, and you will eventually be a worthy partner of the feasts of the gods. And if you don't even take the things which are set before you, but are able even to reject them, then you will not only be a partner at the feasts of the gods, but also of their empire.[84]

Epictetus was one of the greats of the Stoic philosophy, which taught an attitude of noble detachment toward the joys and sorrows of daily life. Here is a Buddhist anecdote with a similar message:

Hira Lal had heard that there was a place called Buddha Nagar where everyone was enlightened. He set out looking for this mythical town. After years of wandering, he came to a river. Across the river was Buddha Nagar. Hira Lal got onto a boat. The cool breeze felt so good. A wave of joy swept through him. At last, he had made it to Buddha Nagar. He congratulated himself on the success of his mission. His patience, his struggles had borne fruit. As he looked around with a sense of satisfaction, his eyes fastened onto a corpse floating away. He looked carefully. Why, it was his own corpse. In a single moment, all his achievements, his virtues, his spirituality, even his making it to Buddha Nagar were gone forever. What a loss! In deep sorrow, he started crying, first slowly and then uncontrollably. Then through his tears, he looked at the corpse a second time only to find that his sorrow and sense of loss too had floated away. An all-enveloping peace descended on him. He was liberated from joy and sorrow.[85]

---

84 'The Internet Classics Archive | The Enchiridion by Epictetus'
<http://classics.mit.edu/Epictetus/epicench.html> [accessed 5 November 2012]
85 'A Discussion on the Essential Buddha Nature of Man'
<http://www.lifepositive.com/spirit/world-

All over the world we see a similar approach, in systems of spirituality and philosophy as diverse as Mahayana Buddhism and Roman Catholicism- both joy and sorrow are to be distrusted or rejected or controlled or transcended. Joy and sorrow, after all, are forms of craving or attachment, which many systems define as the core spiritual problem.

The Cauldron text sees things differently. Not only are joy and sorrow not rejected, they are actually essential- the Cauldrons cannot be "turned" without them. The Cauldron text embraces the passions, but it doesn't stop with that. It asks us to "cook" the passions we experience and transform them into art. In other words, the text's attitude to the emotions is not as much of an outlier as it might first appear. The passions are not simply to be craved and pursued and clung to- they are to be engaged with and then transformed.

This is what makes the Cauldron text so fascinating, beyond its inherent interest to modern pagans and Celtophiles. The Cauldron system is a form of spiritual practice specifically for artists. It was designed by artists to be used by artists, and it is based on doing something that artists do anyway- creating art out of strong emotion. By doing what you already do as an artist *but with a spiritual intention*, you can learn to use your art to fully engage with every emotion you experience, fully integrate it into your interior landscape, and transform it into a work of truth and beauty without getting trapped or damaged by it.

Ultimately, the Cauldron system is just as aware of the problem of emotion as any other system of spiritual practice, but it approaches the solution from a different angle. It is not actually unique in this approach. There is a form of Hinduism known as Bhakti, which is based on passionate emotional worship of a particular deity. There is also a sect of Hinduism known as

---

religions/buddhism/zen/bodhidharma.asp> [accessed 5 November 2012]

Shakta, whose adherents worship the Hindu mother goddess as the primary deity. Shaktas believe that the world of ephemeral phenomena we live in, which other Hindu sects identify as Maya or "illusion," is in fact the *lila* or "play" of the Divine Mother. Instead of Maya, Shaktas speak of Maha Maya or "Mother Illusion." Like all other major Hindu sects, the Shakta sect aims to see past the Illusion and achieve Moksha or liberation. Unlike many of the other Hindu sects, they don't reject the Illusion as something bad; instead they think of it as the act of a mother playing with her infant children until they are mature enough to put the toys aside themselves. This isn't the same mentality as our Cauldron text, but it shares with it a generally positive attitude toward the sorrows and joys of human life. Sections of the Cauldron text- particularly those dealing with "divine joy"- bear a resemblance to Bhakti, and you might be able to deepen your practice by reading a little about what Bhaktas do. Of course, you could learn a lot more by studying about early Irish Christianity, because that's what those passages in the text actually refer to- but as someone interested in Celtic spirituality, you've probably already done that!

The word used for "sorrow" in this text is "brón," which the Electronic Dictionary of the Irish Language defines as "sorrow, grief, grieving, lamentation; distress, burden." The word used for "joy" is "failte," which eDIL defines as "happiness; joy; bliss; rejoicings; welcoming" or "greeting; salutation," pointing out that the word was "(o)ften used of spiritual joy and eternal bliss" during the Old Irish period.

So, sorrow is that which burdens us and makes us grieve, while joy is that which we welcome or which gives us spiritual bliss. Most people naturally flee from sorrow and chase after joy, which is exactly why both are considered a spiritual problem by most traditions. Because we cannot successfully evade sorrow or hold on to joy, the natural tendency to flee one and chase the other leads to constant suffering.

Artists (out of what you might call professional necessity!) have always known that either sorrow or joy could get the creative juices flowing and produce artistic inspiration- "turning the Cauldron" as our text would have it. Unfortunately, this awareness has led many artists to accept or even to cultivate an emotionally-unbalanced approach to life, often with self-destructive results. The Cauldron system takes the basic understanding that both sorrow and joy can turn the cauldrons, and gives us a tool for doing so in a conscious, fully-engaged way that gives us the best opportunity for creating art out of our emotions without destroying ourselves in the process. The end-result is not only art but spiritual practice.

Another point we should note is that the fili of medieval Ireland were not known for writing poetry about their personal emotions. The works of the fili are preserved mostly in books called *duanaire*, which were kept by the chiefs and kings who were their primary patrons. Almost every single poem in a *duanaire* is about how great the chief or king is, in highly stereotyped language- the king is brave, fierce in battle, beloved by the ladies, feared by his enemies, and (hint, hint) extremely generous to poets. Most of the Gaelic poetry we have from the era of the fili is of this type, and it's pretty dull reading. Even after the fili began to lose their status as the Gaelic lordships declined, the poetry of the bards who served clan chiefs was equally stereotyped, the main difference being the use of less complex metrical structures. It is only after the decline of the clan system that Gaelic poetry starts to get personal, with the result that a song by a village bard from the nineteenth century usually makes for much better poetry than a poem by a king's fili from a few centuries before, other than the sheer sound-beauty of the fili's complex poetic forms.

Some scholars have assumed that the fili actually didn't write much personal poetry because that wasn't their job. Others have assumed that they probably did, but they did it on their spare time and such poems didn't make it into the official *duanaire*. If we pay attention to the Cauldron text, it would seem that the fili probably wrote a great deal of personal poetry and did so in a systematic way as part of their formal training. Such poems were not part of the fili's official duties, so they didn't get included in the *duanaire*- but they were probably very important to the fili themselves, who considered the act of writing these poems to be part of their professional and spiritual education.

Because the official poetry of the fili didn't have much to do with their own joys and sorrows, you can probably learn more about what their "personal" poetry was like from Gaelic folk songs than from their praise poems to the ruling chiefs. In fact, any album of Gaelic folk songs you can find will have clear examples of most of the specific categories of joy and sorrow described in the Cauldron text. The metrical forms used by the village bards would have seemed simplistic to the elite fili, but the treatment of the emotions was probably much the same.

So, how did the poets "cook" their emotions and transform them into poetry? The text tells us- through the method of Incubation, as confirmed by both the *Memoirs of the Marquis of Clanricarde* and by Martin Martin of Skye. When assigned a particular poetic topic by his instructor (for instance, "the sorrow of longing") or when overwhelmed by one of these powerful emotions in daily life, the poet would retire to a dark cell and remain in the darkness meditating continuously until he had successfully transformed the emotion into a poem.

Martin Martin gives us a few other details of the practice, although they are probably optional rather than essential. One is to wrap something such as a plaid or a blanket around your head to cut off any outside noises and light. The other is to put a stone on your belly to help you regulate your breathing. If you are breathing deeply from the abdomen (as you should be when meditating) your belly should expand as you inhale and contract as you exhale. The stone makes it easier to tell if you are doing this properly.

The basic idea, though, is just to go into the darkness (the metaphorical womb/underworld) and remain there engaging directly with your emotion until inspiration is born within you. The process can be as simple as shutting your door, turning your lights and phone off, and closing your eyes while breathing deeply and meditating. Anything that helps you shut out distracting lights and noises from the outside world would also help. A fili would have actually written the entire poem this way, and if you can do that you should. However, they had extensive training in memorization skills, and you probably don't. If you're a poet or a songwriter, you could continue your Incubation until you get that crucial line or image around which a poem or song is usually built. If you're a painter, you could continue until you get a mental picture of the painting you want to do.

Martin Martin tells us that the poet would spend an entire day on this, and the *Memoirs* tell us the same thing. I'd like to be able to tell you that you can do it in the fifteen minutes before you rush out the door, but you probably can't. You may not need an entire day, but you do need enough time to adopt the attitude of "I'll stay in the darkness for however long it takes until inspiration comes." If it still doesn't come, you can try again next time- but the more time you can give it, the better.

To work with the cauldrons, just make a point of doing this any time your life circumstances cause you to be overwhelmed by powerful emotions. Not only will it improve your ability to tap into your sources of artistic inspiration, it will also make it possible for you to truly engage with your emotions, process them and transform them- a genuinely meditative practice created especially for artists.

The Cauldron text lists four types of sorrow, which Laurie's translation presents in broad terms. Based on the glosses, though, I think Breatnach is correct in his assessment that these sorrows are the three most typical complaints of a young student in the bardic schools- away from the folks back home, homesick for friends and familiar surroundings and nervous about the loyalty of the girlfriend he left behind. Thus, he suffers from grief (as the gloss says, "for his father"), longing (for "people") and jealousy ("after being cuckolded"). Given that the apprentice bards spent entire days in Incubation in total darkness, the "longing" described here may not just be for the poet's own "people" but for any people at all. Mental and physical isolation from others can be extremely trying psychologically, and probably caused the young poets genuine suffering.

The fact that the first three sorrows seem to be drawn from those most likely to afflict the bardic students tells us that the classification into types is somewhat arbitrary. As any artist knows, you can create art from any sorrow or other strong emotion- you don't need to worry about whether it is properly classified as "grief" or "longing."

To these three are added the sorrow of going into exile in some remote place for the sake of God. This would not have been a typical sorrow for the average bardic student, but there seems to have been some overlap between the fili and the monastic poets, many of whom wrote very striking poems about this sort of ascetic practice. So even if the typical fili didn't expect to experience this type of sorrow personally, he would have been aware that you could get good poetry out of it. Some scholars believe that the Irish "desert monk" poems were not all written by genuine exiled monks living in penance on remote islands. After all, how would such a monk have shared his poetry with anyone? It's possible that some or even all of these poems were purely hypothetical, written as "what-if" exercises by student poets or by monks in large, bustling monastic establishments daydreaming about the simple life.

However, even though this extreme form of the fourth sorrow may not have been available to most poets, lesser forms of it would have been. The *Cambrai Homily,* a text from roughly the same era as the Cauldron text, divides martyrdom into three "colors." Red martyrdom is dying for God- an unlikely event in pre-Viking Ireland, since the conversion was essentially bloodless. White martyrdom is exile or extended pilgrimage like the kind described in the text. Finally *glas,* which means "blue-green" or "pale" martyrdom referred to extreme ascetic practices- literally so extreme that they were supposed to give your skin a distinctively blue-green paleness!

Some of the examples given in various texts include sleeping in the presence of a dead body, or spending all night in water, or sleeping on something painful. Although these practices are unquestionably Christian, there are hints of pre-Christian ideas even here. The legendary mad hermit Suibhne Geilt, a pagan king who went mad after insulting a Christian cleric before a major battle, not only lived alone in the wilderness like an exiled monk, he even described himself as being *glas.* Some modern pagans believe *geilta* or "wild men" were a type of ecstatic hermit-prophet in pre-Christian Ireland, perhaps a very rough equivalent of the Indian *sadhu* or ascetic holy man. (The practice of sleeping next to corpses is distinctly similar to some Tantric rituals.)

Another connection with pagan Ireland is in the use of the hunger strike, an ancient Indo-European concept in which you try to blackmail a powerful person into giving you justice by fasting (to death if necessary) on his doorstep. The idea is that if you die he is both dishonored and ritually polluted, so it's a powerful incentive for him to change his ways.

Fasting was a normal part of Christian asceticism everywhere, but in Ireland it was connected directly to the ancient concept of the hunger strike. Some of the saints went so far as to wage hunger strikes against God to get Him to answer their requests, and St. Adomnán combined his own holy hunger strike with a nightly immersion in the Boyne River- home of the goddess Boann and primary sacred river of the pagan Irish and of the bardic guild.

The Irish saints most likely got this idea directly from the fili. According to one of the versions of "The Recovery of the Tain," the great fili Senchán Torpeist "fasted against the race of Fergus" until the spirit of the long-dead Ulster hero appeared and revealed the Tain to him. According to the more common version of the story, the Tain was recovered by Senchán's son Murgein, who sat at Fergus's grave stone and sang to it until Fergus appeared and recited the Tain. The idea of Senchán's fast was that it was a hunger strike against the descendents of Fergus, which would have inflicted the pollution of killing a master poet on them if he had died. To protect his descendents, Fergus was forced to appear and fulfill the poet's request.[86]

This has a couple of interesting implications. For one thing, it connects to the concept of Incubation as a way of acquiring wisdom from the underworld powers or the ancestors. For another thing, it's clearly not an act of worship in the sense of fasting for the love of God- it's an act of blackmail, intended to force the dead to yield the information the poet desires. There are other hints of a cthonic aspect to the spiritual practices of the fili and even to their worship of the goddess Brighid in the legends of Senchán Torpeist, as we will discuss shortly.

These hints of a pagan connection to such a Christian concept as the "blue-green martyrdom" lead me to think that the idea was not completely imported by the Church but may have mingled with preexisting ascetic practices used by the druidic class to either induce prophetic and ecstatic states or to compel the gods to grant a request. Imagine St. Adomnán planning his hunger strike, and a

---

[86] 'The Recovery of the Tain' <http://sejh.pagesperso-orange.fr/keltia/version-en/fallsigud-en.html> [accessed 7 November 2012]

fili telling him "it'll work even better if you do it in the Boyne."

So, I don't think the fourth sorrow should be dismissed by modern pagans as a Christian interpolation. On the other hand, it's probably not something you should trifle with either. Ascetic practices can produce a great deal of spiritual power, but they can also be dangerous both physically and psychologically. Proceed with care.

Breatnach argues that the human joys described by the Cauldron text relate to the life of a bardic student just like the sorrows do. For a young man in the bardic schools, sex would not yet be a matter of marriage and childbirth (except unintentionally). Instead it would be a case of "hooking up" with some interested young lady (or lad) while performing for a local chieftain on the weekends, or possibly even with the chieftain's wife- the gloss insists that "cuckolding" is involved, although the glossator seems to have had an unhealthy obsession with the topic.

For a young man with poetic talent, the chance to become a professional fili would have removed a lot of anxiety about things like getting enough food and warm clothes and adequate medical care- especially since the text puts a lot of emphasis (in contradiction to the *Clanricarde* memoirs) on the idea that poetic training was a way out of poverty for talented young people of low status.

After years spent in training, receiving the full principles of the fili's complex poetic art and prophetic methods must have been extraordinarily satisfying, filling the new professional poet with a sense of personal accomplishment and well-being.

Finally, the poet who experienced the Imbas of mystical inspiration would have been on top of the world, with the benefits of his talent and his chosen path in life confirmed beyond question. So what we have here is a distinctly worldly picture of "the good life" in terms that a modern person can easily relate to- plenty of sex, good health, good food, good clothes, professional success and recognition, and artistic inspiration.

However, the passages on the Imbas merit a closer look. They relate not only to one of the core myths of the bardic guild but to multi-layered metaphors we can use in our own meditative practices. First, the mythic aspect.

The Boyne is the Ganges of pagan Ireland, the ultimate sacred river from which all other rivers in the world are supposed to be derived. In his book *Deep Ancestors*, Serith describes the goddess Boann as a reflex of the much more ancient Proto-Indo-European cow goddess Gwouwinda. Gwouwinda is supposed to be the perfect patriarchal wife and mother- chaste, pure and flawlessly loving.

In Indo-European belief as reconstructed by Serith, the World Tree has a mystical well at its roots containing the fiery waters of Chaos from the watery underworld below. These waters are dangerous and thus taboo, but they also hold the powers of inspiration, wisdom, sovereignty, and many other divine things. The well is guarded by a god whose later reflexes include the Greek Neptune and the Irish Nechtainn- Boann's husband. In Serith's view, Boann's act of adultery with the Dagda is a straightforward violation of her "proper" nature as the idealized wife-goddess Gwouwinda, and that (along with her insistence on walking counterclockwise around the well to curse it) is why she is "punished" by being ripped apart by the well's waters.

I don't believe this is quite right. The bards and fili of medieval Ireland didn't remember Boann as a hated figure of treachery toward her beloved husband- they adored the Boyne (her body) as the source of poetic inspiration or Imbas. They considered the Boyne to be the source of all the rivers in the world. They thought the Salmon of Wisdom from the Well of Segais carried the Imbas up the Boyne. Most crucially, the author of the *Metrical Dindsenchas* states that Boann's name in the Sidhe was "Segais."

The goddess Boann *is* the Well. Her husband Nechtainn, in banning her from approaching it, is banning her from approaching her own self and thus preventing her power from flowing into the mortal world. When the Dagda seduces her, he sets off the act of rebellion in which she deliberately walks counterclockwise around the Well to magically dissolve the boundaries holding it in place.

This is not an act of treachery but of rebellion and self-sacrifice. Although Boann is torn to pieces, the waters flood out into the mortal world and create the Boyne and all other sacred rivers, bringing tremendous benefit to the human race. As a dismembered and "dead" (although not truly dead) goddess, Boann's activity is henceforth restricted- the river Boyne is not going to just get up and walk around. However, the Dagda has a daughter named Brighid- who must be either Boann's daughter or stepdaughter, since Boann is sometimes described as the Dagda's wife- and Brighid becomes the fire to Boann's water. In all the lore associated with Brighid, she is identified with either fire or the sun.

When one of Brighid's sunbeams strikes the plants along the Boyne, the dead goddess's power bubbles up on them and they become infused with Imbas. Brighid, in a sense, is the "new Boann," even taking on her white cow, who is supposed to travel around with Brighid on Imbolc eve. Brighid is capable of operating actively in the world as Boann no longer is.

Now, on to the metaphors. Of course, the Boyne is a real river, but it is much more than that too, as we know from the *Metrical Dindsenchas:*

Banna is her name from faultless Lough Neagh:
Roof of the Ocean as far as Scotland:

Lunnand she is in blameless Scotland--
The name denotes her according to its meaning.

Severn is she called through the land of the sound Saxons,
Tiber in the Romans' keep:
River Jordan thereafter in the east
and vast River Euphrates.

River Tigris in enduring paradise,
long is she in the east, a time of wandering
from paradise back again hither
to the streams of this Sid.

Boand is her general pleasant name
from the Sid to the sea-wall;
I remember the cause whence is named
the water of the wife of Labraid's son.[87]

The Welsh bard Taliesin described the *awen* as a river: "The Awen I sing,/ From the deep I bring it,/ A river while it flows..."[88]

One way to think of this passage and its glosses is to think of the Boyne as the flow or "river" of thought. When the fire of Brighid's inspiration strikes the flowing river of your thoughts, the Imbas bubbles up inside you. This image is key to the actual practice of Imbas Forosnai. In this book, I will treat the flow of thought during Imbas Forosnai as being equivalent to the Boyne, the light of inspiration as being Brighid's *tein fesa* or "fire of knowledge," and the hypnagogic images and phrases that float up out of the stream of consciousness as the bubbles of Imbas. When the fire of Brighid meets the river of thought, you get the Imbas.

---

[87] 'Dindshenchas Boand' <http://www.shee-eire.com/Magic&Mythology/Myths/Tuatha-De-Danann/Dindshenchas-Boand/Page1.htm> [accessed 6 November 2012]

[88] 'Four Ancient Books of Wales: U. Poems Relating to the Life and Opinions of Taliessin.: XC. Hostile Confederacy. Book of Taliessin VII.' <http://www.sacred-texts.com/neu/celt/fab/fab105.htm> [accessed 27 October 2012]

As such, we should never think of Boann as some sort of traitorous version of the chaste Gwouwinda, but more as a "Celtic Prometheus" who brought the divine power of consciousness into the mortal realm.

Esoteric texts, however, frequently have more than one layer of hidden or implied meaning. In the article "Speckled Snake, Brother of Birch: *Amanita Muscaria* Motifs in Celtic Legends," Erynn Rowan Laurie and Timothy White argue that the Imbas was ingested in the form of some kind of entheogen, possibly the *amanita muscaria* mushroom, and that images such as the Salmon eating the hazels at the Well of Segais are coded references to this practice.[89]

As speculative and unprovable as that certainly is, the Cauldron text does tell us that the Imbas is found in plants that grow along the river Boyne. Any time a source tells you that the magic is stored in some plants down by the river, it seems to me that the use of a natural hallucinogen is not a far-fetched interpretation. However, the method in this book will work without chewing any potentially dangerous mushrooms.

Finally, we have "divine joy," which the medieval glosses specifically associate with the wonder-working powers of great saints like Colm Cille. It is tempting to see this as an interpolation, because there are three secular sorrows and the divine sorrow of ascetic practice. If this was originally a druidic version of ascetic practice such as the behaviors of the *geilta*, it would be exactly paralleled by the three secular joys of sex, well-being and artistic accomplishment and the divine joy of the Imbas. Three secular sorrows and three secular joys; one divine sorrow and one divine joy. That could possibly have been the original pre-Christian version of the system.

---

[89]'Dindshenchas Boand' <http://www.shee-eire.com/Magic&Mythology/Myths/Tuatha-De-Danann/Dindshenchas-Boand/Page1.htm> [accessed 6 November 2012]

One reason for thinking this might be the case is the traditional division of Irish music into the "Ábhann Tríreach" or "Triple Strain," defined by the late Alexei Kondratiev as follows:

goltraí: laments, music for weeping, intended to provoke emotion and sympathy
geantraí: dance music, lively tunes, music for good feelings, creating a happy and optimistic mood
suantraí: lullabies, various kinds of slow airs, music for sleep, which calmed the emotions and promoted relaxation[90]

Boann is supposed to have been the inventor of the Triple Strain, and her lover the Dagda had a magic harp that performed all three types of music when he was in the camp of the Fomorian giants. The goltrai made them weep, the geantrai made them laugh, and then the suantrai lulled the Fomorians into a magic sleep.[91] If you think of the suantrai as "meditative" music, we have a very similar pattern to the Cauldron text- three sorrows and a "meditative" sorrow, three joys and a "meditative" joy. I'm inclined to think the division of sorrows and joys in the Cauldron text is directly related to the Triple Strain concept, especially since the deities mentioned in connection with the Triple Strain are the father and the mother or stepmother of the goddess of poetry.

However, the text as we have it considers the Imbas to be a secular joy, and treats divine joy as a distinct category. For our purposes, I am treating the Imbas as an oracular/ecstatic/artistic power with mystical overtones, and I take "divine joy" to refer to the highest levels of religious ecstasy, vision and mystical union.

---

90 'Pre-Christian Heritage' <http://homepage.eircom.net/~shae/chapter11.htm> [accessed 9 November 2012]

91 For anyone interested in the parallels some see between the Three Cauldrons and Hinduism's three gunas or "qualities," the three Strains are actually a much closer fit.

In the early Irish church, these were sometimes associated with the goddess Brighid's successor, Saint Brighid of Kildare. One of the hagiographies of the saint describes her as the sun above the City of Heaven and adds "may we reach that unity which exists forever and ever."[92] Then we have a prayer to St. Brighid with a verse reading "Lead us to the eternal kingdom/ The dazzling resplendent sun."[93]

So, in the not-entirely-orthodox enthusiasm of the early Irish Christian, Brighid is the sun above the City of Heaven, and the sun is the mystic "unity which exists forever and ever" (the Kingdom of God), and St. Brighid has the power to lead us to this mystical sun, which is ultimately herself.

To a modern "Celtic Christian," divine joy could be mystical union with God, and St. Brighid the intermediary who can lead us to this blessed state. To a modern pagan, "divine joy" could be ecstatic union with Brighid as Goddess. To a universalist practitioner of either religion, there is not necessarily any fundamental difference between these two points of view.

Most of the Cauldron text is put into the mouth of the mythical poet Amergin, the archetypal fili. One long section near the end is instead attributed to Néde mac Adnai. This seems potentially significant, so it makes sense to find out who Néde was. Néde mac Adnai was the upstart fili in the *Colloquy of Two Sages*, who attempted to usurp the bardic chair until bested by Ferchertne. According to Rhys:

O'Curry gives a tragic instance: the poet Néde mac Adnai, in order to obtain possession of the throne of Connaught, asked an impossible request of the king, who was his own father's brother and named Caier. When the king declared his inability to accede to his demand the poet made the refusal his excuse for composing on the king what was called in Irish an air or der, written later aor, 'satire,' which ran approximately thus:--

---

92 From O'Duinn's *The Rites of Brigid,* pg 7, quoting Stokes.
93 From Wright's *Brigid, Goddess, Druidess and Saint,* pg 84.

Evil, death, short life to Caier!
May spears of battle wound Caier!
Caier quenched, Caier forced, Caier underground!
Under ramparts, under stones with Caier!

O'Curry goes on to relate how Caier, washing his face at the fountain next morning, discovered that it had three blisters on it, which the satire had raised, to wit, disgrace, blemish, and defect, in colours of crimson, green, and white. So Caier fleeing, that his plight might not be seen of his friends, came to Dun Cearmna (now the Old Head of Kinsale, in county Cork), the residence of Caichear, chief of that district. There Caier was well received as a stranger of unknown quality, while Néde assumed the sovereignty of Connaught. In time, Néde came to know of Caier being there, and rode there in Caier's chariot. But as Néde approached Caier escaped through his host's house and hid himself in the cleft of a rock, whither Mede followed Caier's greyhound; and when Caier saw Néde, the former dropped dead of shame...[94]

This is obviously not a satire in the modern sense, because there isn't a hint of wit about it- it's just straight-up black magic, for the purpose of staging a coup d'etat against the legitimate king. Néde mac Adnai wasn't just a fili, but a hated variation on the fili- a professional satirist misusing the magic powers of poetry for his own selfish purposes. The entire section beginning with "I proclaim the Cauldron of Motion:/ Understanding grace,/ Filling up with knowledge" is put into the mouth of this sinister character. This tells me that the verse in question is primarily about power- the power of the Cauldron, and the power it can give you. These were, after all, Néde mac Adnai's prime concerns.

In any case, the section does tell us some very interesting things. One is that the Cauldron brews a drink made out of "the waters of enlightenment" and the Imbas of the Boyne. Serith discusses the attempts by the different Indo-European peoples to make an

---

[94]'Chapter XI: Folklore Philosophy' <http://www.sacred-texts.com/neu/cfwm/cf205.htm> [accessed 7 November 2012]

earthly equivalent of the drink from the Well of Wisdom. The nature of the drink varied depending on the region. When they reached the Indian subcontinent, the early Vedic Indo-Europeans started making it with a local hallucinogenic plant they called Soma. In the Celtic regions, it seems to have been generally mead or beer, or honeyed beer, or some mixture of these in milk. (The Gaelic prayer called "The Invocation of the Graces," which was supposed to have been spoken by Brighid, describes a drink of "fiery water" made of an alcoholic drink mixed with milk.) There's a reference in one of the Fianna stories to the poets dispensing prophecy after drinking alcohol, and St. Brighid was credited with several beer-related miracles. There is also an Irish bardic poem from around the same era as the Cauldron text that refers to poetry as being simultaneously a "fair woman" or "beautiful maiden" (most likely Brighid) and a drink of mead.[95]

So, I think we can assume that Irish poets in search of the Imbas were not averse to looking for it in a pint of beer or mead. Whisky didn't exist yet when this text was composed, but its Gaelic name of *uisge bheatha* or "water of life" does suggest the waters of the Well.

The other interesting point about this verse is the reference to the Cauldron's protecting power or "Brig." This word, which means either "power" or "height" or "exaltation," is also found in the name of the goddess Brighid. *Cormac's Glossary* says that the poets worshiped Brighid because of the protection she gave them. As we will discuss in the next chapter, this protection was associated with a little-known "dark goddess" aspect of Brighid, a patron of the sometimes-abusive bands of poets known as the

---

[95] 'Goddesses in Celtic Religion — Cult and Mythology: A Comparative Study of Ancient Ireland, Britain and Gaul' <http://theses.univ-lyon2.fr/documents/lyon2/2009/beck_n#p=0&a=top> [accessed 27 August 2013]

Great Bardic Institution, who would travel from king to king making exorbitant demands backed up by the threat of satire. No doubt this was a version of Brighid near and dear to Néde mac Adnai.

wisdom

Most modern pagans have interpreted "Brighid the Woman-Poet," goddess of the fili according to *Cormac's Glossary*, as having the same gentle and sweet character we associate with St. Brighid of Kildare and with the Brighid of traditional Irish and Scottish lore. However, Brighid appears to have been an extraordinarily multifaceted goddess, truly a female equivalent of the omnicompetent Lugh, and that means she has many aspects- including a largely unrecognized darker side.

Cesiwir Serith's reconstruction of Proto-Indo-European religion in his book *Deep Ancestors* posits eight Indo-European goddesses (or possibly "goddess-types" with multiple local forms and names). Leaving aside his reconstructed Indo-European names for these goddesses, we have:

The Mare Goddess- dangerous, sexually voracious or transgressive in some way, symbolized by a mare, this goddess grants the drink of Sovereignty to worthy kings. The classic Irish examples would include Macha, Maeve and the Morrigan.

The Cow Goddess- chaste, pure, loving and approachable, this goddess gives fertility and well-being of all kinds. Boann, whose name means "white cow" or "she who has white cows" is an Irish example.

The Dawn Goddess- a beautiful young maiden.

The Daughter of the Sun- who is the sister as well as the wife of one of a pair of divine Twins.

The Hearth Goddess- whose cult is domestic, overseen by the women of the house, and epitomized by a priesthood of "vestal virgins" tending an eternal flame.

The River Mother- the Land goddess of the tribal territory, symbolized by a river. Again, Boann is an example- but so is the Morrigan.

The Goddess of Death- who leads the dead to the underworld.

The Earth Mother- whose body is the landscape. Anu is an Irish example, as in the hills known as the "Paps of Anu," but we are also told that Anu is one of the "Three Morrigans."

At least in a Celtic context, I think some of these goddess-types actually overlap. There isn't really a clear distinction between the Mare Goddess, the River Goddess, the Death Goddess and the Earth Mother- the Morrigan in her various forms is all of those goddesses at once. Boann is an Earth Mother, a River Mother, and a Cow Goddess.

The ancient devotees of Brighid seem to have seen her as being capable of fulfilling all possible goddess functions. She travels around the world with a magical red-eared white cow on the eve of Imbolc, blessing the homes and livestock of her devotees. This makes her a Cow Goddess, and in this form she is portrayed as being kind, infinitely loving, sexually chaste, capable of granting fertility- all classic characteristics of the Cow goddess. Because most of the surviving Brighid folklore comes from the rural peasantry of the Gaelic areas, this is the form of Brighid most modern pagans are familiar with. However, it was never her only aspect.

As St. Brighid, she is supposed to have been born at dawn on the threshold of a house, neither inside nor outside. This makes her a Dawn Maiden. In this form she is represented as a *brideog* or "young Brighid" during the Imbolc festivities. The *brideog* is either represented by an image of a baby, or by a pretty adolescent girl or girls, or by a group of cross-dressing boys. The cross-dressing probably represents the "neither this not that" liminality of dawn and the threshold.

Brighid is repeatedly associated with the sun in Gaelic prayers and lore, including the story of St. Brighid hanging her cloak on a sunbeam and other descriptions of Brighid as the sun above the City of Heaven. In Indo-European religion, the Daughter of the Sun is usually portrayed as the Sky God's daughter and as the wife of one of the Twins. Brighid the goddess is the daughter of the Dagda, who has Sky God characteristics such as his club and his epithet of "All-Father". The Dagda is also the father of Aengus by Boann, making Aengus Brighid's brother or half-brother. Aengus is not described as a twin in Gaelic lore, but his Welsh cognate Mabon[96] is. In Scottish lore, Brighid is sometimes described as the lover of Aengus. So, as the daughter of a Sky God and the sister and lover of one of the divine Twins, Brighid is also a Daughter of the Sun.

The traditional hearth prayers and ritual in Gaelic folklore were almost always dedicated to Brighid and performed by the woman of the house, and Brighid had her own sect of "vestal virgins" who tended her eternal flame at Kildare. So Brighid is also the Hearth Goddess.

Brighid's River Mother connections are less immediately apparent, but the river Braint in Anglesey is thought to be named after a Brythonic cognate of the goddess.[97] Brighid's Earth Mother connections can be seen in the fact that she was thought to give the seasons their functions and to oversee the transition from winter to spring.

So, just as Lugh as the "Samildanach" or "god who is good at everything" was able to perform the functions of all of the Celtic

---

[96] Whose name matches Aengus's epithet of "Mac ind Oic." Both refer to the ancient Celtic god Maponos, the "Young Son."

[97] 'Brigit in Wales: Sant Ffraid' <http://www.brigitsforge.co.uk/st_ffraid.htm> [accessed 7 November 2012]

gods at once, Brighid seems to have been seen as a goddess who could perform the functions of all of the Indo-European goddess types through her various aspects- and as such, she may have been seen less as "a goddess" by her devotees and more as "the Goddess"- a nearly all-powerful female deity.

Until recently, I thought there was one exception. All of Brighid's forms and functions seemed to take the characteristics of what Serith called the Cow goddess- purity, compassion, love and light. There seemed to be no version of Brighid as the Mare goddess- cthonic, dark and dangerous.[98] The only hint of such an aspect was in an enigmatic comment by Lady Gregory that Brighid's face was supposed to have a beautiful side and a repulsive side, and vague Scottish folklore to the effect that the seemingly opposed goddesses known as Bride and the Cailleach were really the same entity.

We know from Cormac's Glossary that the Irish poets worshiped Brighid as "Brighid the Woman-Poet," and in the absence of further details most people assumed this aspect of Brighid had the same qualities as the Brighid we know from the Imbolc festivities and from Gaelic prayer. But those aspects of Brighid have to do with her role as a Cow goddess and a Hearth goddess. Brighid the Woman-Poet could have a very different nature, as can be seen in the legends associated with Senchán Torpeist.

In a Scottish folktale preserved in fragmentary form in the repertoire of Cape Breton storyteller Joe Neil MacNeil, Senchán himself is barely remembered, and the story focuses on his wife as the leader of a kind of bardic mafia called the "Cleith Sheanachair" or "Senchán's Band." This wandering tribe of poetic extortionists travels from place to place bankrupting kings with their excessive demands for royal hospitality and generosity,

---

[98] Although, oddly enough, when St. Brighid was adopted into Haitian Voodoo as Maman Brigitte, she became just such a goddess, the wife of the cemetery god.

backed up by the threat of satire. Clearly this tale is told from the point of view of the kings, so Brighid and the poets are not going to come off well in this story. But then again, complaints about artists receiving government grants are still with us today!

The really important point here is the title and characteristics given to Brighid the Woman Poet- characteristics preserved, so far as I know, only in this one obscure Scottish folk tale. These reverse all of Brighid the Cow Goddess's usual functions.

This Brighid is not associated with a red-eared white cow, but a red-eared white horse. She is not associated with light and life, but with a "pig that has never been born." According to Serith, pigs are always cthonic symbols. If pigs come originally from the land of the dead (as they do in the Mabinogion) then a pig that has never been born must still belong to the realm of the dead. This Brighid does not respect the proper order of things like a Cow goddess. Instead, she demands "blackberries in January"- a phrase that can easily be read as "spring before Imbolc." In other words, this Brighid is not content to begin her reign with the Gaelic spring at the traditional time- she wants it *now*. As such, she oversteps her proper authority, just like the extortionist fili she oversees and protects.

Finally, this Brighid is given the title "Great Bríd of the Horses." She's a Mare Goddess, not a Cow Goddess. She is propitiated by the king and sent away with offerings of blackberries in January, pork from a pig that has never been born (because it was delivered through Caesarean section) and a ride on a red-eared white horse. In the story, the king can only deliver the red-eared white horse to Great Bríd of the Horses by taking a regular white horse and painting its ears with the blood of the pig. So, a cthonic pig sacrifice is what gives Brighid the power to take on the identity of her usual opposite, the Mare, with connotations of death and sexuality and raw power.[99]

---

[99] 'Tales Until Dawn: The World of a Cape Breton Gaelic Story-Teller - Joe

What's the point of all this? That the legends of Senchán and Great Bríd of the Horses are essential to truly understanding the Cauldron text, what it means by "wisdom," and what it intends by spirituality. Great Bríd of the Horses is associated with a pig and with the knowledge of the underworld, just like the Welsh muse Cerridwen. Her Cauldron of Wisdom (just like the Cauldron the Welsh bard Taliesin tries to steal from Annwm) is in the underworld realm, not the heavens. This only makes sense, because the Well of Segais is also cthonic. Its Indo-European prototype, according to Serith, was at the roots of the World Tree. The *Metrical Dindsenchas* tells us that the Well "gushed forth every kind of mysterious evil./ There was none that would look to its bottom but his two bright eyes would burst".[100] This exactly matches Serith's assertion that the original Indo-European well contained the waters of Chaos, which had to be brought up into the Cosmos in a controlled way to make use of their power.

Wisdom, in other words, is a dark thing, and the aspect of Brighid concerned with wisdom is a dark goddess. And what exactly is this darkness? It is the darkness of Incubation where the poet composes poetry and communes with the gods; it is is the womb of the goddess; it is the underworld cave of St. Patrick's Purgatory; it is the Cauldron. That's why this version of the

---

Neil MacNeil, John Shaw - Google Books' <http://books.google.com/books?id=pBNn8NWrRtgC&pg=PA49&lpg=PA49&dq=%22Great+Br%C3%ADd+of+the+Horses%22&source=bl&ots=98zBHuOMqR&sig=lMKvXs8Zak0wUNF1O178L4zLEc8&hl=en&sa=X&ei=tseZUJ7-H8_jqAHT64CwCw&ved=0CDcQ6AEwAQ#v=onepage&q=%22Great%20Br%C3%ADd%20of%20the%20Horses%22&f=false> [accessed 7 November 2012]

100'Dindshenchas Boand' <http://www.shee-eire.com/Magic&Mythology/Myths/Tuatha-De-Danann/Dindshenchas-Boand/Page1.htm> [accessed 7 November 2012]

Cauldron system does not place three cauldrons at three different points in the body like chakras or like the Chinese dantiens, even though I can see the validity in those approaches. In my view, the three cauldrons are all ultimately one Cauldron, and they are all in the underworld. They are all in the *broinn* or "belly/womb". They are all inside the dark goddess until she gives birth to the master poet.

Even though the aspect of Brighid associated with poetry is the little-known Dark Brighid called Great Bríd of the Horses, she is not truly distinct from any of the more familiar and lovable aspects of the goddess- at least not in my opinion. Brighid's absorption of all of the goddess-types into a single all-powerful figure tells me that her ancient devotees saw her as containing everything implied by the word Goddess, whether light or dark. Most of them would have approached her in her light form, but the poets also worshiped her dark form as the source of their wisdom. When the Cauldron text speaks of wisdom, it means the wisdom of the underworld. When the Cauldron generates the principles of all arts, it draws them from the stored knowledge of the dead. That's why Amergin performs for Eber Donn.

However, the ultimate power of the Cauldron is not dark in nature, except in the sense that numinous awe is always terrifying.

When the Cauldron text tells us that divine grace fills up the Cauldron and fully activates it, and that this is an example of joy coming from outside the poet to fully actualize his powers, we can think of this as almost a reverse of eastern concepts in which the kundalini power rises up through the chakras to achieve mystical union at the crown chakra.

Instead of the power rising up from below, it flows down from above. God's grace (for a Celtic Christian) or Brighid's celestial fire (for a pagan) or Brighid as the Sun of Heaven (for either) pours divine grace, joy, love and light into the Cauldron, fully activating and transforming the dark power of the Well of Wisdom so that it starts gushing out the flow of Imbas- giving birth to enlightenment. When this occurs, the power from the Cauldron reverses and flows upward- like the Well of Wisdom overflowing in a sudden, terrifying roar of water.

human sorrow

Now that we've examined the nature of the three cauldrons that cook the nine emotions, let's look at how some of the historical fili approached the nine sorrows and joys.

The first three sorrows listed by the Cauldron text are "human" sorrows, emotions that everyone experiences whether they practice any form of spirituality or not. The first of these human sorrows is the sorrow of longing, as expressed in the great saint Colm Cille's poem of sorrow on leaving Ireland for exile in the Hebrides:

Delightful to be on the Hill of Howth
Before going over the white-haired sea:
The dashing of the wave against its face,
The bareness of its shores and of its border.

Delightful to be on the Hill of Howth
After coming over the white-bosomed sea;
To be rowing one's little coracle,
Ochone! on the wild-waved shore.

Great is the speed of my coracle,
And its stern turned upon Derry:
Grievous is my errand over the main,
Travelling to Alba of the beetling brows.

My foot in my tuneful coracle,
My sad heart tearful:
A man without guidance is weak,
Blind are all the ignorant.

There is a grey eye
That will look back upon Erin:
It shall never see again
The men of Erin nor her women.

I stretch my glance across the brine
From the firm oaken planks:

Many are the tears of my bright soft grey eye
As I look back upon Erin...

Melodious her clerics, melodious her birds,
Gentle her youths, wise her elders,
Illustrious her men, famous to behold,
Illustrious her women for fond espousal.

It is in the West sweet Brendan is,
And Colum son of Criffan,
And in the West fair Baithin shall be,
And in the West shall be Adamnan.

Carry my greeting after that
To Comgall of eternal life:
Carry my greeting after that
To the stately king of fair Navan.

Carry with thee, thou fair youth,
My blessing and my benediction,
One half upon Erin, sevenfold,
And half upon Alba at the same time.

Carry my blessing with thee to the West,
My heart is broken in my breast:
Should sudden death overtake me,
It is for my great love of the Gael.

(From: *Selections from Ancient Irish Poetry,* translated by Kuno Meyer, 1911)

The sorrow of longing can also be seen in legends such as *The Fate of the Children of Tuirenn*. Tuirenn was supposed to have been Brighid's first huband, so his children may also have been her children. In revenge for their murder of his father Cian, the god Lugh forced them to wander the world performing a series of nearly impossible tasks for him until they died.

Since Lugh's name may refer to lightning and Tuirenn's name definitely means "thunder," this legend may reflect tensions between followers of the older Celtic thunder god Taranis and the newer god Lugus- although no one can say for sure. If you want to explore the sorrow of longing, you can incubate and compose a poem or other piece of art from the perspective of the children of Tuirenn going into exile on their doomed quest, separated from their father Tuirenn and their mother Brighid.

If you would prefer a more sympathetic set of protagonists, another option would be the *The Fate of the Children of Lir*, who were forced to wander the earth as swans because of the jealousy of Aoife.

The next sorrow in the Cauldron text is the sorrow of grief, as expressed in one of the masterpieces of early Irish literature, the *Lament of the Old Woman of Beare*:

Ebb-tide to me as of the sea!
Old age causes me reproach.
Though I may grieve thereat--
Happiness comes out of fat.

I am the Old Woman of Beare,
An ever-new smock I used to wear:
To-day--such is my mean estate--
I wear not even a cast-off smock.

It is riches
Ye love, it is not men:
In the time when we lived
It was men we loved.

Swift chariots,
And steeds that carried off the prize,--
Their day of plenty has been,
A blessing on the King who lent them!

My body with bitterness has dropt
Towards the abode we know:
When the Son of God deems it time
Let Him come to deliver His behest.

My arms when they are seen
Are bony and thin:

Once they would fondle,
They would be round glorious kings.

When my arms are seen,
And they bony and thin,
They are not fit, I declare,
To be uplifted over comely youths.

The maidens rejoice
When May-day comes to them:
For me sorrow is meeter,
For I am wretched, I am an old hag.

I hold no sweet converse,
No wethers are killed for my wedding-feast,
My hair is all but grey,
The mean veil over it is no pity.

I do not deem it ill
That a white veil should be on my head:
Time was when many cloths of every hue
Bedecked my head as we drank the good ale.

The Stone of the Kings on Femen,
The Chair of Ronan in Bregon,
'Tis long since storms have reached them.
The slabs of their tombs are old and decayed.

The wave of the great sea talks aloud,
Winter has arisen:
Fermuid the son of Mugh to-day
I do not expect on a visit.

I know what they are doing:
They row and row across
The reeds of the Ford of Alma--
Cold is the dwelling where they sleep.

'Tis 'O my God!'
To me to-day, whatever will come of it.
I must take my garment even in the sun:
The time is at hand that shall renew me.

Youth's summer in which we were
I have spent with its autumn:
Winter-age which overwhelms all men,
To me has come its beginning.

Amen! Woe is me!
Every acorn has to drop.
After feasting by shining candles
To be in the gloom of a prayer-house!

I had my day with kings
Drinking mead and wine:
To-day I drink whey-water
Among shrivelled old hags.

I see upon my cloak the hair of old age,
My reason has beguiled me:
Grey is the hair that grows through my skin--
'Tis thus I am an old hag.

The flood-wave
And the second ebb-tide--
They have all reached me,
So that I know them well.

The flood-wave
Will not reach the silence of my kitchen:
Though many are my company in darkness,
A hand has been laid upon them all.

O happy the isle of the great sea
Which the flood reaches after the ebb!
As for me, I do not expect
Flood after ebb to come to me.

There is scarce a little place to-day
That I can recognise:
What was on flood
Is all on ebb.

(From: *Selections from Ancient Irish Poetry,* translated by Kuno Meyer, 1911)

This poem imagines the ancient goddess known as the Cailleach lamenting the loss of her youth and power and becoming a nun. Another example of the sorrow of grief can be found in Deirdre's lament for the Sons of Uisneach:

Long is the day without Usnagh's Children;
It was never mournful to be in their company.
A king's sons, by whom exiles were rewarded,
Three lions from the Hill of the Cave.

Three dragons of Dun Monidh,
The three champions from the Red Branch:
After them I shall not live--
Three that used to break every onrush.

Three darlings of the women of Britain,
Three hawks of Slieve Gullion,
Sons of a king whom valour served,
To whom soldiers would pay homage.

Three heroes who were not good at homage,
Their fall is cause of sorrow--
Three sons of Cathba's daughter,
Three props of the battle-host of Coolney.

Three vigorous bears,
Three lions out of Liss Una,
Three lions who loved their praise,
Three pet sons of Ulster.

That I should remain after Noisi
Let no one in the world suppose!
After Ardan and Ainnle
My time would not be long.

Ulster's high-king, my first husband,
I forsook for Noisi's love:
Short my life after them,
I will perform their funeral game.

After them I will not be alive--
Three that would go into every conflict,
Three who liked to endure hardships,
Three heroes who never refused combat.

O man that diggest the tomb,
And that puttest my darling from me,
Make not the grave too narrow,
I shall be beside the noble ones.

(From: *Selections from Ancient Irish Poetry,* translated by Kuno Meyer, 1911)

This poem can be found in *The Exile of the Sons of Uisneach*, and you can explore the sorrow of grief by incubating a poem or other piece of art based on this tale. Another option would be *The Death of Aoife's Only Son,* which tells the tale of how the hero Cuchulain killed his own child.

The next sorrow mentioned by the Cauldron text is heartbreak or jealousy, depending on how you interpret what the text is trying to say. When the sea goddess Fand lost her lover Cuchulain to his mortal wife Emer, she is said to have spoken the following poem expressing both heartbreak and jealousy:

'Tis I who must go on this journey,
Our great necessity were best for me;
Though another should have an equal fame
Happier for me could I remain.

Happier it were for me to be here,
Subject to thee without reproach,
Than to go, — though strange it may seem to thee, —
To the royal seat of Aed Abrat.

The man is thine, O Emer,
He has broken from me, O noble wife.
No less, the thing that my hand cannot reach,
I am fated to desire it.

Many men were seeking me
Both in shelters and in secret places;
My tryst was never made with them,
Because I myself was high-minded.

Joyless she who gives love to one

Who does not heed her love;
It were better for her to be destroyed
If she be not loved as she loves.

With fifty women hast thou come hither,
Noble Emer, of the yellow locks,
To overthrow Fand, it were not well
To kill her in her misery.

Three times fifty have I there,
— Beautiful, marriageable women, —
Together with me in the fort :
They will not abandon me.

(From: *The Lamentation of Fand* in *The Poem-Book of the Gael*, edited by Eleanor Hull)

This poem can be found in the story called *The Sickbed of Cuchulain and the One Jealousy of Emer.* You could explore the sorrow of heartbreak and jealousy by creating a piece of art from the perspective of either Emer or Fand.

Divine Sorrow

In the Cauldron text, "divine sorrow" refers to the practice of going into exile for the sake of God, as the early Gaelic saints did in imitation of the Egyptian desert monks. Not having any desert near at hand, they usually chose either isolated spots deep in the forest or islands in the middle of the Atlantic ocean:

Shall I launch my dusky little coracle
On the broad-bosomed glorious ocean?
Shall I go, O King of bright Heaven,
Of my own will upon the brine?

Whether it be roomy or narrow,
Whether it be served by crowds of hosts--
O God, wilt Thou stand by me
When it comes upon the angry sea?

(From: *Selections from Ancient Irish Poetry,* translated by Kuno Meyer, 1911)

In the remote island outposts they referred to as "deserts," the monks must often have been at the mercy of the sea:

A great tempest rages on the Plain of Ler, bold across its high borders
Wind has arisen, fierce winter has slain us; it has come across the sea,
It has pierced us like a spear.

When the wind sets from the east, the spirit of the wave is roused,
It desires to rush past us westward to the land where sets the sun,
To the wild and broad green sea.

When the wind sets from the north, it urges the dark fierce waves
Towards the southern world, surging in strife against the wide sky,
Listening to the witching song.

When the wind sets from the west across the salt sea of swift currents,
It desires to go past us eastward towards the Sun-Tree,
Into the broad long-distant sea.

When the wind sets from the south across the land of Saxons of mighty shields,

The wave strikes the Isle of Scit, it surges up to the summit of Caladnet,
And pounds the grey-green mouth of the Shannon.

The ocean is in flood, the sea is full, delightful is the home of ships,
The wind whirls the sand around the estuary,
Swiftly the rudder cleaves the broad sea.

With mighty force the wave has tumbled across each broad river-mouth,
Wind has come, white winter has slain us, around Cantire, around the land of Alba,
Slieve-Dremon pours forth a full stream.

Son of the God the Father, with mighty hosts, save me from the horror of fierce tempests!
Righteous Lord of the Feast, only save me from the horrid blast,
From Hell with furious tempest!

(From: *Selections from Ancient Irish Poetry,* translated by Kuno Meyer, 1911)

Although the concept of "divine sorrow" in this sense is clearly Christian, ascetic practices may have been part of the pre-Christian religion as well, particularly in connection with magic and rituals intended to control the powers of the otherworld. As we discussed earlier, fasting was probably a pagan practice as well as a Christian one, although performed with the intention of blackmailing the spirits rather than purifying one's own spirit.

The *geilta* or prophetic madmen of Gaelic legend are the closest "pagan" equivalent to the hermit-monks of Irish lore. The most famous of the *geilta* was Suibhne Geilt, a king who went mad after a battle and fled to the forest where he lived in the trees like a bird. Suibhne was driven mad by the curse of a saint whom he had offended, but in most other legends it is the Morrigan who inflicts this state on warriors overwhelmed by the horror of battle. They remain closely connected to her ever afterward. Throughout the Ulster Cycle of Irish legend, the "madmen of the glen" scream out whenever the Morrigan appears on the battlefield. Suibhne's birdlike characteristics could also be a reference to the Morrigan's raven form.

Clearly, the Christian version of divine sorrow is completely different from the pagan version, which is bloody and dark in nature. This verse could be said to express the feeling I'm talking about:

Horrible are the huge entrails which the Morrigan washes.
She came to us from the edge of a spear, 'tis she that egged us on.
Many are the spoils she washes, terrible the hateful laugh she laughs.
She has flung her mane over her back--it is a stout heart that will not quail at her:
Though she is so near to us, do not let fear overcome thee!

(From: *Selections from Ancient Irish Poetry,* translated by Kuno Meyer, 1911)

From a pagan perspective, the grim nature of this emotion is no reason to shy away from what it may have to teach us. In spiritual traditions from other parts of the world, such as Tantra and Chöd, meditation on horrific images or in places such as graveyards and cremation grounds is used to transcend ordinary human consciousness and the limitations of the ego.

That the *geilta* concept involves something similar can be seen in the fact that Suibhne Geilt's story has a Welsh parallel in the tale of Myrddin Wyllt. Myrddin Wyllt, just like Suibhne, went mad after a battle, fled into the wilderness, and became a prophet. The name "Myrddin" is the Welsh version of "Merlin" and "Wyllt" is the Welsh equivalent of "Geilt" or "wild." In other words, the madness and horror of the war goddess is how the legendary Merlin acquired his powers.

Meditation on horrific imagery such as the many descriptions of the Morrigan washing the gory clothes of the slain, could be seen as a pagan practice of "divine sorrow" for the purpose of turning the cauldrons and invoking art and inspiration- especially (and this would be similar to Chöd practice) if your visualize the Morrigan washing out your own bloody clothes, the ravens of the battlefield feasting on your flesh, and so on. You could also read the story of *Suibhne Geilt* and create a work of art from Suibhne's perspective.

human joy

The human joys in the Cauldron text begin with erotic yearning, arguably the most ambivalent of all joyful emotions. Between the joy of yearning and the sorrow of jealousy and heartbreak there is a very fine line, and this is reflected in many of the Irish poems about love, which convey both sides of the emotion at the same time.

Do you remember that night
When you were at the window,
With neither hat nor gloves
Nor coat to shelter you ?
I reached out my hand to you,
And you ardently grasped it,
I remained to converse with you
Until the lark began to sing.

Do you remember that night
That you and I were
At the foot of the rowan-tree,
And the night drifting snow ?
Your head on my breast.
And your pipe sweetly playing ?
Little thought I that night
That our love ties would loosen !

Beloved of my inmost heart,
Come some night, and soon,
When my people are at rest.
That we may talk together.
My arms shall encircle you
While I relate my sad tale,
That your soft, pleasant converse
Hath deprived me of heaven.

The fire is unraked,
The light unextinguished,
The key under the door,
Do you softly draw it.
My mother is asleep,

But I am wide awake ;
My fortune in my hand,
I am ready to go with you.

(From: *The Poem-Book of the Gael*, edited by Eleanor Hull)

The feeling of erotic yearning was sometimes projected onto the idealized image of the fairy woman, as in these verses from *Laegh's Description of Fairy-Land*:

A vat there is of heady mead
Being dispensed to the household;
Still it lasts, in unchanged wise,
Full to the brim, everlastingly.

There is a maiden in the noble house
Surpassing the women of Eire,
She steps forward, with yellow hair,
Beautiful, many-gifted she.

Her discourse with each in turn
Is beauteous, is marvellous,
The heart of each one breaks
With longing and love for her.

(From: *The Poem-Book of the Gael*, edited by Eleanor Hull)

The references to a beautiful fairy woman and a vat of mead bring to mind the poem about the Spirit of Poetry as a "fair woman" serving mead. This supernatural woman could be a form of Brighid as the goddess of poetry, or a *leannan sidhe* or fairy lover. Every poet was supposed to have one, and the fairy lover could be either male or female. Of course, the *leannan sidhe* was supposed to be vampiric, slowly draining the poet's vitality in exchange for inspiration, but such are the risks of the profession.

One way to work with this joy would be to create art inspired by the imagined or visualized form of your personal erotic ideal. Another would be to create a piece inspired by one of the Irish legends that have to do with this emotion, such as *The Pursuit of*

Diarmaid and Grainne or the tale of the Dagda's meeting by the river with the Morrigan:

The Dagda had a house in Glen Edin in the north, and he had arranged to meet a woman in Glen Edin a year from that day, near the All Hallows of the battle. The Unshin of Connacht roars to the south of it. He saw the woman at the Unshin in Corann, washing, with one of her feet at Allod Echae (that is, Aghanagh) south of the water and the other at Lisconny north of the water. There were nine loosened tresses on her head. The Dagda spoke with her, and they united. "The Bed of the Couple" was the name of that place from that time on. (The woman mentioned here is the Morrigan.)

(From: *The Second Battle of Mag Tuired,* translated by Elizabeth A. Gray)

Of course, the Morrigan is not the only goddess associated with the Dagda in this way. The Dagda also had an affair with the river goddess Boann, which led to her fateful visit to the Well of Segais. This tale would be another appropriate option for a piece of art inspired by erotic yearning.

In the Cauldron text, the joy of health and prosperity refers to the carefree mindset of the young poet who has enough to eat, a place to sleep and any health care he might need upon attaining the status of professional poet. Sadly, none of these things are likely to attend the practice of poetry in these degenerate times. Nevertheless, it is still the case that it is much easier to think about things like poetry when you don't have to think about where your next meal is coming from or how you're going to get that infection treated.

For anyone who has experienced real poverty, the feeling of having enough money on hand to stop worrying for a while is so liberating it can actually induce a mild state of ecstasy. This emotion of total well-being is not limited to financial prosperity, because it can be glimpsed in some of the Irish nature poetry:

Summer has come, healthy and free,
Whence the brown wood is aslope;

The slender nimble deer leap,
And the path of seals is smooth.

The cuckoo sings sweet music,
Whence there is smooth restful sleep;
Gentle birds leap upon the hill,
And swift grey stags.

Heat has laid hold of the rest of the deer--
The lovely cry of curly packs!
The white extent of the strand smiles,
There the swift sea is.

A sound of playful breezes in the tops
Of a black oakwood is Drum Daill,
The noble hornless herd runs,
To whom Cuan-wood is a shelter.

Green bursts out on every herb,
The top of the green oakwood is bushy,
Summer has come, winter has gone,
Twisted hollies wound the hound.

The blackbird sings a loud strain,
To him the live wood is a heritage,
The sad angry sea is fallen asleep,
The speckled salmon leaps.

The sun smiles over every land,--
A parting for me from the brood of cares:
Hounds bark, stags tryst,
Ravens flourish, summer has come!

(From: *Selections from Ancient Irish Poetry,* translated by Kuno Meyer, 1911)

With some of these poems, you can sense that the poet has just survived yet another harsh winter and is positively ecstatic to see the sun shining:

Summer-time, season supreme!
Splendid is colour then.
Blackbirds sing a full lay

If there be a slender shaft of day.

The dust-coloured cuckoo calls aloud:
Welcome, splendid summer!
The bitterness of bad weather is past,
The boughs of the wood are a thicket.

Panic startles the heart of the deer,
The smooth sea runs apace--
Season when ocean sinks asleep,
Blossom covers the world.

Bees with puny strength carry
A goodly burden, the harvest of blossoms;
Up the mountain-side kine take with them mud,
The ant makes a rich meal.

The harp of the forest sounds music,
The sail gathers--perfect peace;
Colour has settled on every height,
Haze on the lake of full waters.

The corncrake, a strenuous bard, discourses,
The lofty cold waterfall sings
A welcome to the warm pool--
The talk of the rushes has come.

Light swallows dart aloft,
Loud melody encircles the hill,
The soft rich mast buds,
The stuttering quagmire prattles.

The peat-bog is as the raven's coat,
The loud cuckoo bids welcome,
The speckled fish leaps--
Strong is the bound of the swift warrior.

Man flourishes, the maiden buds
In her fair strong pride.
Perfect each forest from top to ground,
Perfect each great stately plain.

Delightful is the season's splendour,

124

Rough winter has gone:
Every fruitful wood shines white,
A joyous peace is summer.

A flock of birds settles
In the midst of meadows,
The green field rustles,
Wherein is a brawling white stream.

A wild longing is on you to race horses,
The ranked host is ranged around:
A bright shaft has been shot into the land,
So that the water-flag is gold beneath it.

A timorous, tiny, persistent little fellow
Sings at the top of his voice,
The lark sings clear tidings:
Surpassing summer-time of delicate hues!

(From: *Selections from Ancient Irish Poetry,* translated by Kuno Meyer, 1911)

This type of joy in physical well-being and the natural world can be found in any of the Fianna legends, but particularly in the bard Ossian's defense of the pagan lifestyle to St. Patrick in the *Colloquy of the Ancients*. The best way to work with this emotion is probably to compose nature poetry or create other works of art inspired by nature, but the *Colloquy* could also be a source of inspiration.

There are not many examples in Irish poetry of the joy of artistic or professional accomplishment, unless you count the vast numbers of praise-poems to the ruling chiefs and provincial kings. This particular joy is said to be "the joy of acquiring the principles of poetry and prophesy after long study," as expressed by Néde mac Adnai in *The Colloquy of the Two Sages:*

I am son of Poetry,
Poetry son of Scrutiny,
Scrutiny son of Meditation,
Meditation son of Lore,

Lore son of Enquiry,
Enquiry son of Investigation,
Investigation son of Great-Knowledge,
Great-Knowledge son of Great-Sense,
Great-Sense son of Understanding,
Understanding son of Wisdom,
Wisdom, son of the three gods of Poetry.

(From: *The Colloquy of the Two Sages*, translated by Whitley Stokes)

The Colloquy of the Two Sages is the story of how Néde mac Adnai became so full of himself after "acquiring the principles of poetry and prophesy" that he challenged an older and more experienced fili to a duel of bardic knowledge. As Néde mac Adnai is supposed to be the author of a section of the Cauldron text, this tale would be a very appropriate choice for investigating this emotion.

The final joy is the joy of Imbas, the mystical power of inspiration or ecstasy. This power was supposed to be derived from the Boyne River, which is to say that it derives ultimately from the Well of Segais.

Both poets refer to this legend extensively in the *Colloquy of the Sages*:

The old poet spake to the young poet : —

'Who is this sage around
whom is wrapped the robe of splendour ?
and whence comes he?"

The young poet answered :

"I spring from the heel of a wise man,
From the meeting-place of wisdom I come forth;
From the place where goodness dwells serene.
From the red sunrise of the dawn I come,
Where grow the nine hazels of poetic art.
From the wide circuits of splendour

Out of which, according to their judgment, truth is weighed.
There is a land where righteousness is instilled,
And where falsehood wanes into twilight.
There is a land of varied colours
Where poems are bathed anew.
And thou, O well-spring of Knowledge, whence comest thou?"

"Well can the answer be given:
I move along the columns of age,
Along the streams of inspiration,
Along the elf-mound of Nechtan's wife.
Along the forearm of the wife of Nuada,
Along the fair land of knowledge
The bright country of the sun;
Along the hidden land which by day the moon inhabits;
Along the first beginnings of life."

(From: *The Colloquy of the Two Sages*, in *The Poem-Book of the Gael*, edited by Eleanor Hull)

The "nine hazels of poetic art" are the trees that grow around the Well of Segais. (Could this be a reference to the nine sorrows and joys that turn the cauldrons?) Boann was Nechtan's wife, so the "elf-mound of Nechtan's wife" would be Brugh na Boinne, the great Neolithic monument on the Boyne River. "The forearm of the wife of Nuada" is the Boyne itself, since Boann's husband is sometimes named as Nechtan and sometimes as Nuada, and the Boyne is made of her dismembered body.

The actual experience of Imbas can result in visions and other mystical experiences, as in this vision of the Tuatha de Danann:

White shields they carry in their hands,
With emblems of pale silver;
With glittering blue swords,
With mighty stout horns.

In well-devised battle array,
Ahead of their fair chieftain
They march amid blue spears,
Pale-visaged, curly-headed bands.

They scatter the battalions of the foe,
They ravage every land they attack,
Splendidly they march to combat,
A swift, distinguished, avenging host!

No wonder though their strength be great:
Sons of queens and kings are one and all;
On their heads are
Beautiful golden-yellow manes.

With smooth comely bodies,
With bright blue-starred eyes,
With pure crystal teeth,
With thin red lips.

Good they are at man-slaying,
Melodious in the ale-house,
Masterly at making songs,
Skilled at playing *fidchell*.

(From: *Selections from Ancient Irish Poetry,* translated by Kuno Meyer, 1911)

Another way to experience Imbas is through the vision of the fairy woman, inviting the dreamer on a voyage to the otherworld:

Once when Bran, son of Feval, was with his warriors in his royal fort, they suddenly saw a woman in strange raiment upon the floor of the house. No one knew whence she had come or how she had entered, for the ramparts were closed. Then she sang these quatrains to Bran while all the host were listening.

I bring a branch of Evin's apple-tree,
In shape alike to those you know:
Twigs of white silver are upon it,
Buds of crystal with blossoms.

There is a distant isle,
Around which sea-horses glisten:
A fair course against the white-swelling surge--
Four pedestals uphold it.

A delight of the eyes, a glorious range
Is the plain on which the hosts hold games:

Coracle contends against chariot
In Silver-white Plain to the south.

Pedestals of white bronze underneath
Glittering through ages of beauty:
Fairest land throughout the world,
On which the many blossoms drop.

An ancient tree there is in bloom,
On which birds call to the Hours:
In harmony of song they all are wont
To chant together every Hour.

Colours of every shade glisten
Throughout the gentle-voiced plains:
Joy is known, ranked around music,
In Silver-cloud Plain to the south.

Unknown is wailing or treachery
In the homely cultivated land:
There is nothing rough or harsh,
But sweet music striking on the ear.

Without grief, without gloom, without death,
Without any sickness or debility--
That is the sign of Evin:
Uncommon is the like of such a marvel.

A beauty of a wondrous land,
Whose aspects are lovely,
Whose view is wondrous fair,
Incomparable is its haze.

Then if Silverland is seen,
On which dragon-stones and crystals drop--
The sea washes the wave against the land,
A crystal spray drops from its mane.

Wealth, treasures of every hue
Are in the Land of Peace-- a beauty of freshness:
There is listening to sweet music,
Drinking of the choicest wine.

Golden chariots on the plain of the sea
Heaving with the tide to the sun:
Chariots of silver on the Plain of Sports,
And of bronze that has no blemish.

Steeds of yellow gold are on the sward there,
Other steeds with crimson colour,
Others again with a coat upon their backs
Of the hue of all-blue heaven.

At sunrise there comes
A fair man illumining level lands:
He rides upon the white sea-washed plain,
He stirs the ocean till it is blood.

A host comes across the clear sea,
They exhibit their rowing to the land:
Then they row to the shining stone
From which arises music a hundredfold.

It sings a strain unto the host
Through ages long, it is never weary:
Its music swells with choruses of hundreds--
They expect neither decay nor death.

Many-shaped Evna by the sea,
Whether it be near, whether it be far--
In which are thousands of many-hued women,
Which the clear sea encircles.

If one has heard the voice of the music,
The chorus of little birds from the Land of Peace,
A band of women comes from a height
To the plain of sport in which he is.

There comes happiness with health
To the land against which laughter peals:
Into the Land of Peace at every season
Comes everlasting joy...

(From: *Selections from Ancient Irish Poetry,* translated by Kuno Meyer, 1911)

The vision of the fairy woman leads to *immrama* or *echtrae,* a fantastic voyage across the otherworldly ocean from one strange island to another as in *The Voyage of Bran.* Arguably, the last lines of the Cauldron text actually refer to such a vision.

Poetry or other artwork based on the joy of Imbas should ideally be inspired by the direct experience of the Imbas itself, rather than being mediated through a story or other source. However, studying and visualizing legends of the *immrama* might be a way to trigger the Imbas.

divine joy

The Cauldron text makes some sweeping claims for divine joy, or *déoldae*:

> Divine joy, however, is the coming of holy grace into the Cauldron of Motion so that it turns upright, granting wisdom in both secular and sacred matters, the power of prophesy, and the ability to work wonders and give wise judgments.

Only the saints and gods of Irish legend display powers like that, such as St. Patrick when he said his famous *Lorica* and magically disguised both himself and his companions as deer:

I arise to-day
Through the strength of heaven:
Light of sun,
Radiance of moon,
Splendour of fire,
Speed of lightning,
Swiftness of wind,
Depth of sea,
Stability of earth,
Firmness of rock.

I arise to day
Through God's strength to pilot me:
God's might to uphold me,
God's wisdom to guide me,
God's eye to look before me,
God's ear to hear me,
God's word to speak for me,
God's hand to guard me,
God's way to lie before me,
God's shield to protect me,
God's host to save me...

(From: *Selections from Ancient Irish Poetry,* translated by Kuno Meyer, 1911)

"Wisdom in both secular and sacred matters" could include esoteric lore such as the traditional colors of the twelve winds, a strange concept that must surely have occurred to a poet in some ecstatic vision:

King who ordained the eight winds
advancing without uncertainty, full of beauty,
the four prime winds He holds back,
the four fierce under-winds.

There are four other under-winds,
as learned authors say,
this should be the number, without any error,
of the winds, twelve winds.

King who fashioned the colours of the winds,
who fixed them in safe courses,
after their manner, in well-ordered disposition,
with the varieties of each manifold hue.

The white, the clear purple,
the blue, the very strong green,
the yellow, the red, sure the knowledge,
in their gentle meetings wrath did not seize them.

The black, the grey, the speckled,
the dark and the deep brown
the dun, darksome hues,
they are not light, easily controlled.

King who ordained them over every void,
the eight wild under-winds;
who laid down without defect
the bounds of the four prime winds.

From the East, the smiling purple,
from the South, the pure white, wondrous,
from the North, the black blustering moaning wind,
from the West, the babbling dun breeze.

The red, and the yellow along with it,
both white and purple;
the green, the blue, it is brave,
both dun and the pure white.

The grey, the dark brown, hateful their harshness,
both dun and deep black;
the dark, the speckled easterly wind
both black and purple.

Rightly ordered their form,
their disposition was ordained;
with wise adjustments, openly,
according to their position and their fixed places.

The twelve winds,
Easterly and Westerly, Northerly and Southerly,
the King who adjusted them, He holds them back,
He fettered them with seven curbs.

King who bestowed them according to their posts,
around the world with many adjustments,
each two winds of them about a separate curb,
and one curb for the whole of them.

King who arranged them in habitual harmony,
according to their ways, without over-passing their limits ;
at one time, peaceful was the space,
at another time, tempestuous.

(From: *The Poem-Book of the Gael*, edited by Eleanor Hull)

In Christian terms, the coming of "divine joy" in its fullest sense would render the recipient into a wonder-working saint such Colm Cille or St. Brighid of Kildare. In pagan terms, such a power would be equivalent to that of the archetypal bards Taliesin or Amergin. To invoke the power of divine grace- even if in diluted form!- create art inspired by the all-powerful saints or bards of the Celtic tradition.

Imbas Forosnai

According to *Cormac's Glossary* as translated by Whitley Stokes:

Imbas forosna, 'Manifestation that enlightens': (it) discovers what thing soever the poet likes and which he desires to reveal.(2) Thus then is that done. The poet chews a piece of the red flesh of a pig, or a dog, or a cat, and puts it then on a flagstone behind the door-valve, and chants an incantation over it, and offers it to idol gods, and calls them to him, and leaves them not on the morrow, and then chants over his two palms, and calls again idol gods to him, that his sleep may not be disturbed. Then he puts his two palms on his two cheeks and sleeps. And men are watching him that he may not turn over and that no one may disturb him. And then it is revealed to him that for which he was (engaged) till the end of a nómad (three days and nights), or two or three for the long or the short (time?) that he may judge himself (to be) at the offering... Patrick banished that and the Tenm láida 'illumination of song,' and declared that no one who shall do that shall belong to heaven or earth, for it is a denial of baptism.[101]

According to Nora Chadwick's research into Imbas Forosnai, it is probably not the case that St. Patrick was responsible for banning this practice. Cormac was just venturing a guess as to why the practice was no longer common in his own time, and the fact that offerings to pagan gods were involved presented one plausible explanation. Even Cormac says that other forms of oracular practice were not banned because they did not involve any such heathen offerings. So it is not that the practice of Incubation is inherently evil or forbidden, it is just that Christians are obviously not supposed to make offerings to "idol gods." A Christian reader interested in practicing Incubation obviously could do so without performing such an offering, since Incubation is defined by meditation in silence and darkness rather than by the heathen offerings of Imbas Forosnai.

---

[101] 'Searching for Imbas: Imbas Forosnai by Nora K. Chadwick' <http://searchingforimbas.blogspot.com/p/imbas-forosnai-by-nora-k-chadwick.html> [accessed 8 November 2012]

Chadwick also found numerous references to Imbas Forosnai without the use of Incubation or "mantic sleep." However, the close connection between the Incubation form of Imbas Forosnai and the Cauldron of Incubation makes this version the important one for us.

Here's an alternative translation of the same passage by Meyer:

The Imbas Forosnai sets forth whatever seems good to the seer (file) and what he desires to make known. It is done thus. The seer chews a piece of the red flesh of a pig, or a dog, or a cat, and then places it on a flagstone behind the door. He sings an incantation over it, offers it to the false gods, and then calls them to him. And he leaves them not on the next day, and chants then on his two hands, and again calls his false gods to him, lest they should disturb his sleep. And he puts his two hands over his two cheeks till he falls asleep. And they watch by him lest no one overturn him and disturb him till everything he wants to know is revealed to him, to the end of nine days, or of twice or thrice that time, or, however long he was judged at the offering.

The contradictions between the two passages are explained by the obscurity and difficulty of the original text, but it is possible to outline a series of steps:

1- The poet chews on a piece of raw flesh, without swallowing. According to Chadwick, this represents partaking of the food of the otherworld.
2- The poet makes an offering of the raw flesh to the gods, with a sung incantation.
3- The poet sings another incantation while gazing down into his open palms.
4- The poet covers his eyes (either with his palms as described by Cormac or by wrapping something around his face as described by Martin Martin) and enters Incubation in the "dark cell."
5- The poet remains in the darkness until he receives Imbas in a dream or vision- even if it takes several days.

Aspects of this cannot realistically be done in the modern world. We obviously don't eat dogs or cats, many people don't eat meat at all, and chewing raw pork can cause fatal food poisoning. Laurie has suggested that the offering was never really raw flesh in the first place, and that the poet is really chewing an entheogen such as a dried piece of hallucinogenic mushroom. I'm not going to tell you not to experiment with that if you're determined to do so, but please be very careful. There are legally-available entheogens you could use, but you'll have to research safe dosages and sources yourself. I have not personally found the use of entheogens to be necessary for this practice.

Substituting other items for what was originally an animal sacrifice is a very ancient custom in Hinduism. For instance, non-vegetarian Kali-worshipers sometimes sacrifice animals in Her honor, but vegetarian Kali-worshipers sacrifice pumpkins. Tantric worshipers often use mental substitutions for the physical offerings described in their texts. So there is nothing wrong with making such a substitution, as long as we understand and properly utilize the symbolism involved.

If we look at the types of flesh used in the ancient version of the ritual, we see that the choices are the dog, the cat or the pig. Not just any meat will do- it has to be an animal associated with death and the underworld, because the Incubation ritual is a symbolic descent into the realm of the dead. For a descent into the realm of the dead you need a psychopomp, a guide and protector- and who better than Brighid the Woman-Poet, mythic protector of the bardic class?

The mortal husband of Great Bríd of the Horses was the poet Senchán Torpeist[102], and he was eventually carried away to the underworld by a giant cat. Dogs (among other things) were a symbol of death in Irish lore.[103] We have already seen that the pig

---

[102] Assuming that she can be identified with his wife Brigit, which seems very likely given that her story describes her as the leader of his band of poets and the fact that the names Brigit and Brid are equivalent in Gaelic.
[103] 'Dog: A Celtic Mythological Animal'

is associated with Great Bríd of the Horses, and for a very specific reason- only the blood of "a pig that has never been born" can turn a regular white horse into an otherworldly "white horse with red ears," thus transforming a Cow goddess into a Mare goddess.

In fact, if you look at the three gifts demanded by Great Bríd of the Horses in the story, you can read them as a set of coded instructions for Imbas Forosnai- "If you want Brighid to step outside of her normal functions and powers (like getting blackberries in January or "spring before Imbolc") in order to take you to the underworld, you must offer raw pork flesh ("otherworld food") and she will be able to take on the powers and characteristics of the Mare goddess (as if riding on an otherworldly mare)."[104]

In order to symbolize this entire process, the obvious choice is to offer blackberries. This receives further confirmation from the tale "Does Greth Eat Curds." In the version of this tale given in *Cormac's Glossary,* the second Amergin is described as "gnawing on" curds, garlic, sloes, green leeks, onions, sour apples and blackberries while in his fugue-like silence. In fact, what snaps him out of it is the appearance of Greth on the scene to borrow something from his father, prompting Amergin to speak his first words: "Does Greth eat curds?"

<http://www.celtnet.org.uk/miscellaneous/dog.html> [accessed 8 November 2012]

104 Just to be clear, I'm not saying somebody deliberately encoded this information into the story, although I don't think that's out of the question either. There's a very ancient tradition of expanding the uses of a text through interpretation and commentary. For instance, practitioners of Kaballah will read esoteric meanings into the Torah, practitioners of Tantra will read Tantric layers of meaning into the Vedas, and medieval Catholic monks would read mystical interpretations into seemingly straightforward Biblical passages. The notion that a text can only ever say what it originally said is a peculiarly Protestant one.

If we think of Amergin's fugue as an extended state of Incubation, the question he asks Greth could be read as "Does Greth know how to perform Imbas Forosnai?" Greth does not, but he considers the question so terrifying that he runs off and talks the poet Aithirne into trying to kill the young man with a bill-hook before he says anything else.

So, the simple substitution for the raw flesh offered in the performance of Imbas Forosnai could be blackberries alone, but a more complex version would be a mixture of curds, garlic, sloes, green leeks, onions, sour apples and blackberries. Either way, you don't actually eat the offering- you just chew it up or gnaw on it for a while and then offer it to the gods on your altar. The other option would be to visualize chewing on raw flesh and then leaving it as an offering, without actually chewing on anything.

After the offering comes the first incantation, calling the gods (such as Great Bríd of the Horses) to come and partake of the offering. The second incantation over the palms is for inducing the trance, after which the poet enters the darkness and silence of Imbas Forosnai.

When the ancient fili performed Imbas Forosnai, they delivered the resulting prophecies in the form of poems called *rosc* (plural *rosconna*). A number of these are found in many of the old Irish sagas, but scholars usually decline to translate them because they are multi-layered, filled with double meanings and bizarre images. They are semi-incomprehensible and almost entirely untranslatable. One example is the "Song of Amergin" from the *Book of Invasions*.

I am the wind on the sea (for depth);
I am a wave of the deep (for weight);
I am the sound of the sea (for horror);
I am a stag of seven points (for strength);
I am a hawk on a cliff (for deftness);
I am a tear of the sun (for clearness);

I am the fairest of herbs;
Í am a boar for valour;
I am a salmon in a pool (i.e. the pools of knowledge);
I am a lake on a plain (for extent);
I am a hill of Poetry (and knowledge);
I am a battle-waging spear with trophies (for spoiling or hewing);
I am a god, who fashions smoke from magic fire for a head (to slay therewith);
(Who, but I, will make clear every question?)
Who, but myself, knows the assemblies of the stone-house on the mountain of Slieve Mis?
Who (but the Poet) knows in what place the sun goes down?
Who seven times sought the fairy-mounds without fear?
Who declares them, the ages of the moon?
Who brings his kine from Tethra's house?
Who segregated Tethra's kine?
(For whom will the fish of the laughing sea be making welcome, but for me?)
Who shapeth weapons from hill to hill (wave to wave, letter to letter, point to point)?
Invoke, O people of the waves, invoke the satirist, that he may make an incantation for thee!
I, the druid, who set out letters in Ogham;
I, who part combatants;
I, who approach the fairy-mounds to seek a cunning satirist, that he may compose chants with me.
I am the wind on the sea.

(From: *The Poem-Book of the Gael*, edited by Eleanor Hull)

Historically, Imbas Forosnai was used to answer questions. Though these questions could be quite mundane, there's no reason they couldn't be esoteric too. One way to practice would be to take an image or a question from this mysterious poem and perform Imbas Forosnai to find out what it means. Just don't expect your answers to be the same as anyone else's.

The Gods of Imbas Forosnai

The description of Imbas Forosnai in *Cormac's Glossary* describes the poet calling the gods to him twice- once to partake of the offering (and therefore, presumably, to guide him safely to the underworld to receive the Imbas) and the second time so they don't "disturb his sleep"- more likely so they will grant him the dream-vision he's asking for when he goes into trance.

Unfortunately, Cormac doesn't tell us which gods these are, but Great Bríd of the Horses is certainly a strong candidate. Deities the fili might have invoked during Imbas Forosnai include:

Domnu- The Fomorian mother goddess, about whom little is known. Her name means "The Depths" or "The Abyss." She is the power of the deepest and darkest waters of the ocean and the cthonic realm. The first three lines of the "Song of Amergin" may refer to her or invoke her. This goddess could be seen as an earlier form of the Cailleach, since the Cailleach is described in Scottish lore as being the mother of all the Fomorian giants. Another storm-hag called the Muilerteach is also described in Highland lore, and is strongly associated with the ocean. The Muilerteach has huge tusks and only one eye, and is a fierce, bloodthirsty fighter. If Domnu was invoked during Imbas Forosnai, it would have been for the purpose of inducing trance and accessing the power of the underworld.

Tethra- This Fomorian ocean god is referenced repeatedly in the "Song of Amergin," and may have been invoked for deep trance and access to the underworld.

The Dagda- Brighid's father. A god of druidism and knowledge whose Undry Cauldron can never be emptied.

Boann- River goddess, cow goddess and bringer of consciousness and wisdom to humanity.

The Morrigan- The Morrigan is much more than just a war goddess. Among her many other functions, she appears as a prophetess after the Second Battle of Moytura and as a satirist to Cuchulain in the *Tain Bo Regamna*. As a fili who made her home in the mysterious Cave of Cruachu, the Morrigan's relevance in any prophetic and cthonic ritual should be obvious.

Manannan MacLir- This sea god was often portrayed as a psychopomp, so he may have been invoked to lead the fili safely into the Sea realm.

Fand- Manannan's wife, and the lover of Cuchulain. An example of the *leannan sidhe* concept.

Donn- Or Eber Donn. The brother of Amergin, and the god of the dead or ancestor god of the Gaelic Irish. His house Teach Duinn is either on an island or beneath the waves.

The Tri De Dana- The "three gods of art" must have been an important concept in the pre-Christian Irish religion, but their identities seem to be different in every single source. Sometimes they are Lugh, the Dagda and Ogma, which would make sense as all three of them are also bards. Sometimes they are Brian, Iuchar and Iucharba, Lugh's mortal enemies. Sometimes they are Goibniu, Creidhne and Luchta. Sometimes Danu is their mother, sometimes the Morrigan, sometimes Brighid. Sometimes one of the gods described as a member of the Tri De Dana in one source is described as an ancestor of the Tri De Dana in another source. The lore about the "three gods" is extremely obscure.

Great Bríd of the Horses- Goddess of the bardic order, associated with a red-eared white horse and "a pig that has never been born."

The following poem is from my own practice of Imbas Forosnai, recounting a dream-encounter with the Cailleach:

I have crossed the line. And I have drunk
Too deeply of the strong wine You serve-
Not to those who deserve it, because
What does that mean?- but to those You own.
And I have blazed past the stone doorway
Into the heart of the stone. The moan
Of the cold waters comes crashing in
Across the barrier of my mind,
And I find myself before the Hag.
Her eyes hold horror, but they are wise.
She stirs Her pot. This pit of Hers is
A spiral galaxy made of thoughts.
"The dot at the heart of the whirling
Centuries is the black hole of death,"
She whispers, stirring. "And it is the
Terrible stillness from which the world
Is made. And even I am afraid."

She gives a thin and sinister grin
And I begin to change into some
Bent, crooked form in a storm of lights.
"I have waited here for you for so
Many nights!" She cackles. "But are you
Ready for this? Those waters are not
Just where I do my washing, you know.
You're going down into Death! Going
Down into the power that made time!
Are you ready?" I scream in horror
And sing out flame. The mountain mother
Speaks my name, touches my cheek, and says
"Just let it all out, dearie." I try
To speak, but only fire comes out.
She stirs the pool of the galaxies
As I writhe and shout. New planets form,
Come to life in a storm of colors,
Fade and die with their suns. Like a fish
In a frying pan, I hop and twitch.
And the witch holds up a blazing coal
With an unwholesome grin, then shoves it

In between my eyes. I scream and scream
And start to rise. The drunken numbness
Of power comes flooding angrily
Between my bones. "Maybe a little
Drowning would help you," She says, and moans.

She grabs me by the roots of my hair
And shoves me face-first into the pool
Where the spiral waters turn and turn.
The waters of death where worlds are born.
I feel the mark of the gods in my
Secret womb. I have swallowed a ball
Of fire, I have swallowed a sun.
I have followed the goddess of the
Primal waters to where there is not
Even One. I have swallowed the dark
And I will give birth to words. I have
Become Her cauldron, I have become
Her bliss. I have become the silence
And solitude of the vast Abyss.
And now I rise up through the dark sea
Of my own drowning, until I float
In space. Until I hover before
The ancient Mother and Her shrieking
Face. And when I raise my hands in prayer,
When I dare to praise Her not in spite
Of Her horror, but because She Is,
When I dare to sing a song of love
To that most awesome Power in my
Most terrible fear- She draws me near.
She picks up Her cauldron with both hands
And pours lava into the hollow
Tube of my spine. I begin to shine.

Don't let the dark imagery in this poem give you the wrong impression- the Cailleach is not an "evil" goddess. As important as concepts of moral good and evil are to us humans, they are not applicable to the primeval powers of nature, which create and destroy unceasingly without regard for such categories. Only those who can love the terrible face of the Cailleach can fully understand the beauty of Bride as she brings the spring.

The Cauldron Ritual

A Bardic Mystical Practice

The Cauldron ritual is a form of Imbas Forosnai or bardic mystical practice, using the framework of the Three Cauldrons from the *Cauldron of Poesy* text:

> The Cauldron of Incubation is upright from the moment it is generated. It dispenses wisdom to people as they study in youth.
>
> The Cauldron of Motion, however, magnifies a person after it is turned upright. It is on its side when first generated.
>
> The Cauldron of Wisdom is upside-down when generated. If this cauldron can be turned, it distributes the wisdom of every art there is.

Some people think of the Three Cauldrons as being located in three different areas of the body: the Cauldron of Incubation in the belly, the Cauldron of Motion in the chest and the Cauldron of Wisdom in the head. My preference is to think of the Three Cauldrons as a single Cauldron with three different states of being and three different names. In all three aspects, this Cauldron is located in the *broinn* or "belly/womb."

Whichever approach you take, the Cauldron of Incubation "cooks" the basic skills and techniques of the art you practice. Once you have achieved a level of basic technical skill in your chosen art, the Cauldron of Incubation has done its work.

According to the Cauldron text, everyone can generate and make use of the Cauldron of Incubation, but only about half of the human race is capable of using the Cauldron of Motion. This Cauldron is upside-down in those who lack the artistic temperament or insight to activate it, and on its side in those who have some level of artistic ability. The Cauldron of Motion can be turned upright and fully activated by any powerful emotion, especially the nine emotions listed in the Cauldron text:

Human Sorrows: longing, grief, heartbreak
Divine Sorrow: ascetic religious practice such as solitude, fasting and so forth
Human Joys: erotic yearning, health and prosperity, artistic accomplishment, Imbas (poetic ecstasy)
Divine Joy: spiritual wisdom

If the Cauldron of Motion is fully activated by Divine Joy, it can activate the Cauldron of Wisdom, granting a range of miraculous powers and deep spiritual insight. Full activation of the Cauldron of Wisdom is a godlike state, like that of the archetypal bards Amergin and Taliesin or the wonder-working saints of the early Celtic church. Momentary activation of the Cauldron of Wisdom is much more common, but still life-changing.

The goal of the Cauldron ritual is to turn the Cauldron of Motion upright and activate its power, through the use of Imbas Forosnai, the ancient Irish version of a widespread ancient practice known as "oracular incubation." This is the practice of entering trance or sleep in total darkness and silence to receive a dream or vision. (An *aisling* as it is often called in Irish tradition.)

In my interpretation, the practice of incubation in the "dark cell" is considered equivalent to being in the womb of the goddess Brighid, which is also equivalent to the darkness of the underworld, the depths of the Sea, the depths of the unconscious and the realm of death. At the same time, the practitioner visualizes herself as being "pregnant with poetry," incubating a piece of art in her own *broinn* or "belly/womb." Male practitioners do exactly the same.

The ancient fili or bards used Imbas Forosnai to answer any question they wanted answered, but they also used very similar methods of incubation to compose all their poetry. Both concepts are combined in this Cauldron ritual, which uses the sorrows and joys to turn the Cauldron upright, receive Imbas or poetic ecstasy, and compose a poem (or create any other type of art).

The Cauldron of Motion stays upright only for as long as the Imbas is flowing- after that, it turns back on its side until you activate it again. With repeated practice, you may succeed in activating the Cauldron of Wisdom even if only for a few moments, a spiritual state equivalent to what other traditions would describe as an enlightenment experience. Full activation of the Cauldron of Wisdom is supposed to grant omnicompetence, the ability to perform any art or skill.

The Cauldron Ritual

1- Preparation

1- Prepare a drink to represent the holy drink of Imbas offered to poets by the goddess Brighid. This drink can be honeyed milk, beer, honey-beer, mead, berry-wine, mead mixed with milk, honey-beer mixed with milk, or berry-wine mixed with milk.

2- Prepare a food offering. This can be either a bowl of blackberries, or a mixture containing cheese curds, garlic, sloes, green leeks, onions, sour apples and blackberries.

3- Prepare an altar-space in the area where you will be performing the ritual. The altar can include symbolic representations of whichever deities you intend to call on.

4- Prepare a place where you can lie down, and something to cover your face if you think it would be helpful. Placing a weight on the belly is optional.

It is acceptable to mentally visualize both the offerings and the altar if you prefer. In mental visualization, raw pork can be substituted for the food offering. Do not use raw pork except in visualization, because it is not safe.

2- The Otherworld Feast

1- Drink some of the holy drink. If you choose a drink containing alcohol, don't have enough to make your mind race- just enough to relax you.

2- Chew on the food offering, but do not swallow it. Visualize that you are chewing on the food of the otherworld feast to open the doors of your mind.

3- The Offering

1- Place the chewed-up food offering into a bowl and put it on your altar, along with the rest of the holy drink of Imbas.

2- Kneel or stand in front of your altar, raise your hands in the orans prayer position (with palms facing outward) and recite these lines:

am gaeth i mmuir
am tond trethan
am fuaim mara

You can recite these lines in the original Old Irish, or in English if you prefer.

The first line, "I am a wind on the sea," gives the feeling of diving down into the deep, dark waters. The second line, "I am a wave of the deep," gives a feeling of heaviness. The third line, "I am the sound of the sea," gives the feeling of horror as you enter trance. This feeling of "horror" is not negative or evil- it's the sense of numinous awe as your mind dives deep downward into the unconscious and comes in contact with the vast and primal forces of the divine.

You can visualize yourself as being guided down to the underworld by Great Bríd of the Horses riding a red-eared white horse, or by the Cailleach in her role as the Fomorian mother goddess. Alternatively, you can simply picture yourself descending into darkness and silence without visual images.

Either way, you should continue repeating this chant until you are deeply entranced.

4- The Invocation

1- Gaze down into your open palms and recite an invocation. The invocation you choose is up to you, but here are some options from the "Song of Amergin."

To invoke Brighid in her form as a goddess of limitless compassion and love, chant *am dér gréne* or "I am a tear of the sun".

To invoke Brighid in her form as a goddess of prophesy, power and the underworld, chant *am bri danae* or "I am a hill of Poetry".

These two chants can be used regardless of which emotion you are working with, but you can use these other options if you prefer:

For the emotional agility to work with Longing without being trapped by it, chant *am séig i n-aill* or "I am a hawk on a cliff".

For the strength to work with Grief, chant *am dam secht ndirend* or "I am a stag of seven points".

For the broader perspective needed to transcend Heartbreak, chant *am loch i mmaig* or "I am a lake on a plain".

For the courage to explore the ascetic practices of Divine Sorrow, chant *am torc ar gail* or "I am a boar for valour".

For the beauty and joy of Erotic Yearning, chant *am cain lubai* or "I am the fairest of flowers".

For victory in your daily struggles leading to the joy of Health and Prosperity, chant *am gai i fodb feras feochtu* or "I am a battle-waging spear with trophies".

For the joy of Artistic Accomplishment, chant *am he i llind* or "I am a salmon in a pool".

To invoke and explore the joy of poetic ecstasy or Imbas, chant *am bri danae* or "I am a hill of Poetry".

To invoke and explore Divine Joy, chant *am dér gréne* or "I am a tear of the sun".

2- Continue chanting until you feel ready to enter Incubation.

5- The Incubation

1- Lie down in the place you have prepared, cover or close your eyes, place a weight on your belly to encourage deep breathing if desired, and meditate on the topic you have chosen for your ritual. For instance, if you are exploring the sorrow of grief, you could visualize Brighid keening for her slain son Ruadan after the Second Battle of Moytura. If you are exploring divine joy, you could visualize Brighid as a gloriously radiant solar goddess radiating bliss and ecstasy throughout the universe. The choice of visualization is up to you.

2- Remain in the "dark cell" until your Cauldron of Motion turns and you receive Imbas in some form. This can mean many different things. You could "hear" a line around which you can build a poem or song. You could "see" an image for a painting or sculpture. You could receive a spiritual insight, or an answer to a question. You could experience mystical ecstasy in many forms whether light or dark, calm or wild.

3- When you are finished, write down whatever you have received in a journal or notebook. When you have time, complete the poem or artwork inspired by your experiences in the ritual.

Conclusions

The key point here is that you want to go deeper than your own thoughts, wishes or feelings in order to receive Imbas from the otherworld. This has to be something that happens to you- not just something you imagine.

How can you make this a reality, and how can you tell when you've succeeded? It's actually not that hard. You use the visualization to start your Incubation, and you try to make it as vivid and real as possible- imagine the colors, the textures, the sounds, the smells. But visualization is only your own imagination. It's something you make up yourself.

After a certain point in your Incubation, you will fall into a state of half-sleep known as hypnagogic trance or hypnogogia. Rather than trying to refocus and wake up fully as you would in most traditional forms of meditation, you want to let this happen, because in hypnagogia your ego is no longer in control of what you see and hear. Images- sometimes very vivid ones- will suddenly appear in front of your eyes. Voices will say things to you. This is not psychosis, but a brain-state in-between sleep and waking, a dreaming state you can more easily remember than you can most dreams.

In my interpretation of the Cauldron system, this free-flowing river of consciousness is the mental equivalent of the Boyne. The things you see and hear in this state are considered the "bubbles of Imbas" that arise when Brighid's Fire of Knowledge strikes the waters of the Boyne.

They are direct, prophetic communications containing the wisdom of the underworld. Many of them will make no apparent sense. Some will seem to have some bearing on the topic of your meditation. Some may even be life-changing spiritual revelations.

Every time you complete a meditation, write down anything you saw or heard in this state in a journal. Also write down any dreams you have during the same time-period, particularly those with mythic themes or imagery. In some cases, you will immediately know what the line or image means to you. In other cases, you will suddenly figure it out in a flash of intuition months later as you read through your journal.

Sometimes you may find yourself entering an ecstatic state instead of a hypnagogic state. This could manifest as spontaneous laughter, a sense of energy flowing through you, a sense of divine presence, a feeling of joy far more intense than anything normally experienced in life, or even a vision. The ecstasy is "divine joy" filling up your Cauldron of Motion and turning it fully upright, an important prerequisite to generating the Cauldron of Wisdom. You may not receive any specific oracular information in the ecstatic state, but that doesn't matter- if you really need an answer you can ask again, but the ecstasy is important on its own.

The really important point here is that the things you imagine in your visualization are not very important. Visualization is just a tool. The half-dreams, the dream voices, the ecstasies and the mythic dreams are what you should pay attention to- these are the Imbas.

When you're using Imbas Forosnai as an oracle to resolve a

question in your daily life, you will need to either continue it or repeat it until you receive Imbas with a clear answer to your problem. The Imbas itself doesn't have to be clear- prophesy rarely is. It's likely to be a strange image you will have to interpret. What you need is an interpretation clear enough to give you a direction.

You can also work with this method whenever life causes you to experience powerful emotions such as the four sorrows and the five joys: longing, grief, heartbreak, asceticism, erotic yearning, health and prosperity, artistic accomplishment, the Imbas, and the joy of the divine. For instance, if you experience heartbreak you can shut yourself up in the Incubation and meditate on this emotion until you receive the inspiration to transform your emotion into art. Or, you can engage in ascetic practices such as fasting or celibacy until you receive artistic inspiration.

When you're practicing the Imbas Forosnai to process the joys and sorrows in your inner cauldron, the goal is to receive Imbas relevant to the emotion you are trying to process. This may require several repetitions of the visualization in some cases. You will probably get rapid results in some cases and get stuck for weeks in others. Just be patient and keep working on it; the Imbas will come.

Spiritually speaking, the ultimate goal is to get your Cauldron of Wisdom to turn partially upright at least once. This would be a high-level mystical state far beyond the normal experience of Imbas. A general guideline might be this- "if it's not life-changing, it's not the Cauldron of Wisdom yet."

If you write down the strange things you see and hear when you receive the Imbas and arrange them in some sort of order, you will produce your own very avant-garde modern *roscanna*, at least as obscure as anything an ancient fili could have created. Try it, it's fun!

Summary

Here's a brief summary of the Cauldron ritual for ease of use:

1- Preparation: prepare a holy drink, a food offering, an altar and a place to lie down. All of these elements can be visualized if you prefer, except the place to lie down.
2- The Otherworld Feast: drink some of the holy drink and chew on the food offering without swallowing it.
3- The Offering: leave the rest of the drink and the chewed-up food on the altar. Chant or intone the words "*am gaeth i mmuir, am tond trethan, am fuaim mara*" or "I am a wind on the sea, I am a wave of the deep, I am the sound of the sea" until you feel yourself entering trance.
4- The Invocation: gaze down into your open palms and chant either *am dér gréne* or "I am a tear of the sun," or *am bri danae* or "I am a hill of Poetry".
5- The Incubation: lie down in darkness and silence meditating on the theme of your ritual until you receive Imbas.

Short Version

You can also abbreviate the entire Cauldron ritual by simply lying down, closing your eyes and chanting one of the mantras listed here (either aloud or in your mind) until you receive the Imbas. This method can be just as effective as the longer version once you're used to it, but it will work better if you practice the full ritual from time to time.

appendix- visualizations

Here are some examples of visualizations for the Cauldron ritual, just to give you an idea of the types of scenes you can explore- please don't be bound by them. They are arranged in the form of a connected narrative, but they can be practiced separately or in combination.

I

1- You are lying in your bed in a darkened room when a woman of the Sidhe appears in front of you. She holds up a glowing apple branch and speaks in a voice that sounds like music. "You have been invited by the great goddess Brighid to make the quest of the Three Cauldrons through the underworld realm. Brighid invites you to visit the Well of Segais, the same well that burst out in a rushing torrent and tore Boann to pieces to create the holy Boyne. Brighid would like you to play your harp for Her. Take an apple from the Silver Branch, and let it guide you on your quest." You pull an apple from the branch, and it sings mysterious things to you.

2- You find yourself at the entrance to an ominous-looking cave. You can hear the sound of rushing water just beyond the cave mouth, but you go into the darkness despite your fear. After walking and crawling through a pitch black tunnel for a long time, moving always toward the sound of the water, you come to great cave chamber with ceilings as high as a cathedral. The chamber is lit by a dim glow, and in the center of the floor there is a raging whirlpool. You can just barely see a giant Hag or Cailleach, washing her clothes in the whirlpool and muttering things to herself. Her presence is awesome and terrifying, a raw primordial power as old as the rock. You pause to listen to what she says.

3- You jump or fall in to a whirlpool and it pulls you down. As you pass through the whirlpool, you see a vision: the sacrifice of the Primordial Man, who was ripped to pieces by the raging waves of the otherwordly sea at the dawn of time. As you see this, you feel yourself being ripped apart in the same way. You see the seven elements separating from each other- earth and sea and sun and wind, clouds and stones and the spirit behind all of them- then see their primal energies recombining in fire and thunder and lightning to make a mighty Cauldron. You sense the divine presence of a creator deity putting you together by combining the elements in a unique combination, giving you your own unique qualities and skills. As the deity forges you out of the seven elements, you listen to the mysterious song of creation.

4- You are in the underworld, a strange place of perpetual dawn or twilight, lit by a dim light but still eerily dark. You are on the seashore, looking out over a seemingly endless ocean toward the distant glow of a sun that never rises or sets. There is a boat here waiting for you- a glass coracle, covered in beautiful knot-work designs. You step in to the boat, and the coracle moves under its own power across the underworld sea. As the coracle glides across the dark water, you hear the whispering of the ocean phantoms.

5- You are on the island of the dead, an imposing rock of black stone with a looming, shadowy and ominous-looking hall. This hall is Teach Duinn, the House of Donn. You kneel down, and see that your leg is covered with blue Celtic tattoos. On one knee, you recite a version of the "Song of Amergin", vividly seeing each line as you sing, but your version of the song differs from the original. Where Amergin sang "I am a wind on the sea, I am a stag of seven combats" and other such things, you sing whatever you feel yourself to be. The whispering voices of the dead sing back to you, and you listen to what they have to say.

6- You put on the speckled bird-cloak of the poet and go up to the House of Donn. The gatekeeper is a silent warrior of the dead, holding a thick spear with a broad tip. He will not let you enter, but you display the apple, and he says something to you in the language of the dead. After you hear what he says, you may enter the House of Donn.

7- As you step through the gate into the House of Donn, you see the Cauldron of Incubation in the center of the room, radiating light and fire. Rows of silent warriors sit in the shadows of the hall. Donn sits on his throne. The god of the dead is a somber old warrior, with a hint of his former arrogance and violence still clinging to him- although it has been tempered by death. Nine maidens tend the cauldron, singing the song of the Cauldron of Incubation. You realize that the nine maidens are the true power here, and you recognize them as the great goddesses of Celtic tradition in various forms. The nine maidens are ghostly and distant shapes. The Cauldron sings something to you, and you listen for what it says.

8- The energy of the Cauldron does something to you. You feel yourself changing, and look down at your belly, realizing that you are pregnant- regardless of whether you are female or male. Along with the silent warriors, you see all of your own ancestors who had creative talents in poetry, art or music of any kind, and you realize that your own talent derives from theirs. Donn requests your performance and you display your art for him. You perform the three colors of poetry- white for praise, black for satire and speckled for warning. Donn replies to you in riddling language, and you listen to his words.

9- A goddess steps out from the shadows behind Donn. She reminds you of Brighid, but instead of the kind and endlessly loving energy you associate with that goddess, this goddess has the somber energy of the underworld and eyes that convey a dark power. She holds blackberries in her left hand. At her feet you see a white pig with red ears, and behind her in the shadows you see a white mare whose ears seem to be painted with blood. "I am Great Bríd of the Horses," She tells you. "And you have earned the right to proceed, as you have generated the Cauldron of Incubation." You look down at your pregnant belly and see the upright Cauldron radiating from inside it. The belly of the goddess is also swollen, and you can see yourself inside it as a radiant infant. Great Bríd of the Horses speaks to you, and you listen gratefully to what She says.

II

1- You step into your coracle and set out on the sea. Looking down at your pregnant belly, you can see that the radiant cauldron inside you is now tipped over on its side, and you realize that it has become the Cauldron of Motion. You suffer with intense longing for Brighid. You think of the legend of Brighid's children the Sons of Tuirenn, who had to wander the world to atone for their murder of Lugh's father. You feel as they must have felt, separated from their divine mother. Ahead of you, you see an island with many people on it, wandering and weeping aimlessly.

2- You step into your coracle and set out on the sea. You feel as if your separation from Brighid is the most painful alienation you have ever felt, the alienation of the human from the divine. You think of the legend of Brighid's son Ruadan, who was slain by Goibniu at the Second Battle of Moytura. Ahead of you, you see an island with many people on it, keening and tearing their hair out with grief.

3- You step into your coracle and set out on the sea. You feel heartbroken with loss in your yearning for Brighid. You think of the legend of Brighid's husband Bres, whom she married to bring peace between the gods and the Fomorian giants. You think of the heartbreak Brighid must have felt when she realized that Bres was an untrue king and that the war between gods and giants was inevitable. Ahead of you, you see an island with many people on it, mourning their lost loves.

4- You step into your coracle and set out on the sea. You resolve to suffer for the sake of the divine rather than to simply be overwhelmed by human suffering. You think of the legend of Bride's imprisonment in the mountain of Ben Nevis by the Cailleach, who in some sense is another form of Bride Herself. You realize that Bride's imprisonment every winter is also an incubation as well as a form of exile. You look for an island where you can become a hermit, and find a suitable one after a long search. Here you build a small stone hut and live for a long time in meditation and prayer on the divine in whatever form seems best to you- Brighid, or God or any other divine form.

5- You step into your coracle and set out on the sea. You are filled with life and energy in the form of erotic yearning. You think of the legend of the Dagda and Boann, whose desire for each other brought the waters of wisdom into the mortal world, although they had to deceive Boann's husband Nuada or Nechtainn to be together. You think of the love of Aengus and Bride for each other which brings the spring every year. You see an island ahead of you on which are the most beautiful and desirable men and women you have ever seen. Landing on the island, you are immediately approached by the partner of your choice, who leads you to a beautiful place in which you can enjoy each other for as long as you desire.

6- You step into your coracle and set out on the sea. You are filled with the energy of radiant health and well-being. You think of the legend of Brighid the Healer, visiting the houses of her devotees every Imbolc eve with her red-eared white cow and blessing the pieces of cloth they leave out for her. You see an island ahead of you, on which are healthy and prosperous people, completely free from all anxiety and care. You land on the island, and are greeted by Brighid's father the Dagda, a huge and full-bearded man with a club over his shoulder. Although he appears crude and almost buffoonish at first glance, you sense tremendous wisdom and power in him. Smiling with welcome, he invites you to partake of the otherworldly feast, and you enjoy every kind of delicious food and drink for as long as you please.

7- You step into your coracle and set out on the sea. You can feel that the energies you have been integrating within you are slowly becoming something wonderful, the power and joy of art and prophesy. You think of the legend of Brighid the Smith, forging beautiful new things with fire and hammer, and you realize that you are also being forged into something new. You see an island ahead of you, with nobody on it. You land on the island and stand on the shore, gazing out over the dim sea of early dawn. Remain on the shore of the Island of Prophesy until you receive some form of éicse, the power of poetic prophesy that comes from the waters.

8- You step into your coracle and set out on the sea. You have now become a prophet, and you can feel the glowing cauldron of motion beginning to turn upright within you. You feel awestruck with joy and power. You think of the legend of Brighid the Poetess, inspiring and protecting all artists forever as she has done with you. You see an island ahead of you, on which there is a mighty river flowing down to the sea. Landing on the island, you realize that the river is an otherworldly equivalent of the Boyne itself. Its crystal-clear, beautiful waters reflect the early morning stars, and you realize that the Boyne in its celestial form is the River of Heaven, the Milky Way. Salmon swim and leap in its waters and you can see that each salmon is infused with the power of the Imbas. As you approach the waters, a single beam of light from the rising sun strikes the waters of the Boyne and generates a bubble of pure Imbas. You realize that the waters of the Boyne are the goddess Boann, and the beam of sunlight is Brighid Herself. When the two powers come together, the Imbas is born. The bubble floats through the air to you and you consume it.

9- You step into your coracle and set out on the sea. All the forms of joy and sorrow are combined within you in the love of Brighid, and you feel with great intensity that you want to devote your entire life to this divine joy. You think of the legend of Brighid the Saint, who was said to be an intermediary between human beings and the highest levels of divine unity, like a blazing sun above the City of Heaven. You see an island ahead of you, where the Cauldron of Motion- just like the glowing cauldron in your pregnant belly- is fully upright and supremely radiant. As you land on the island, the Cauldron sings all of the secrets of divine grace.

III

1- You step into your coracle and set out on the sea. The cauldron in your belly is now the Cauldron of Wisdom, but it is upside-down so its extraordinary powers have yet to manifest. However, all of the powers of the Cauldron of Motion are fully activated within you- in effect, the fully upright Cauldron of Motion is identical with the upside-down Cauldron of Wisdom. You see an island ahead of you on which there is a well surrounded by nine hazel trees- the Well of Segais. Nuts drop down from the hazel trees into the waters of the Well, where the Salmon of Wisdom waits to catch and eat them. You realize that the Well is the mystical source of the Boyne river and of all inspiration, and that it will lead you to Brighid. The divine joy you feel on seeing this well is even more intense than anything you have experienced up till now. As your coracle draws closer to the island, you hear the Well singing the secrets of wisdom to you.

2- The god Manannan MacLir comes riding across the sea on his chariot to guide you to shore. He tells you that the streams or rivers you see flowing from the well are the streams of the senses, and that those who drink the water from each of the streams and from the Well of Segais will gain the powers of all the arts. You drink deeply from each stream in turn, moving in a clockwise direction around the well. Clearly experience each sense as you drink from each stream- sight, hearing, taste, touch, smell, speech and thought. Think of each sense as the most amazing gift from the limitless kindness and generosity of Brighid, and feel the joy within you increasing exponentially with every stream. As the power of the water flows through you, it reveals new wisdom.

3- You are standing at the Well of Segais. You look up and see the god Nuada, also known as Nechtainn. He has a shining silver hand and wears a mighty sword. Three cupbearers follow behind him. Nuada tells you that the Cauldron of Motion can be turned by either joy or sorrow, but that the Cauldron of Wisdom can be turned only by ecstatic joy. He bids you to drink from the well, and you do so. The joy that explodes within you when you taste the water of the well causes you to black out completely and transition to a level of reality in which all that exists in front of you is the mighty and transcendent Cauldron of Wisdom, singing with a thousand voices at once of all the secrets of divine reality.

4- The Cauldron of Wisdom in front of you is fully upright and activated. Two mighty powers are pouring into it from the limitless heavens above- the waters of sacred wisdom and the blazing sunbeam of poetic inspiration. Together they merge into the *tein fesa* or Fire of Knowledge, a spiraling whirlpool of sheer power and energy that is somehow both Fire and Water at the same time. You recognize that this spiraling, blazing, liquid energy is the Brig, the divine feminine energy of the universe itself, the Creator and the Creation at the same time, and the divine power within all forms of the divine and all energies of any kind. The ecstatic joy within you reaches still greater heights as the Cauldron of Wisdom sings of the Mysteries of creation.

5- The Cauldron of Wisdom in front of you tips just slightly so that the liquid fire of the *tein fesa* comes pouring out to land on your belly where your internal Cauldron of Wisdom is still upside-down. As the power of the *tein fesa* strikes your belly, you can feel it exerting pressure on your internal cauldron, which begins to spin rapidly inside you. You experience this energy at first as the energy of erotic yearning, but the experience is very different this time than it has ever been before. For one thing, it is no longer explicitly physical- while it retains the quality of an erotic energy, it now feels like the creative impulse of the universe itself rather than an urge for sex as such. For another thing, it is vastly more powerful and joyful. The Cauldron of Wisdom sings of the Mysteries of desire.

6- As the *tein fesa* pours down onto your belly, your internal cauldron spins more and more rapidly. The quality of the energy changes within you, becoming a sense of completely open, free and unrestrained abundance- a divine combination of all health, prosperity, comfort, wealth and generosity in the universe. Recognizing this energy as the kindness of Brighid, your joy becomes boundless. The Cauldron of Wisdom sings of the Mysteries of abundance.

7- As the *tein fesa* pours down onto your belly, your internal cauldron spins more and more rapidly. The quality of the energy changes within you, becoming the power of art and poetry in its most powerful, inspired, prophetic and awe-inspiring sense. You are no longer experiencing joy as something given to you from without, but as the simple fact of what you yourself are. You are a fountain of divine joy, like Brighid Herself. The Cauldron of Wisdom sings of the Mysteries of art.

8- As the *tein fesa* pours down onto your belly, your internal cauldron spins more and more rapidly. The quality of the energy changes within you, and you suddenly see Brighid before you. You can see that She is pregnant, and realize that the baby in Her belly is none other than you. Her beauty, Her compassion and Her power are all infinitely greater than you could even have imagined, and as She smiles gently at you with all the love in the universe, you begin to perform your song for Her out of the spontaneous power of Imbas.

9- As you perform a song for Brighid, three glowing drops of Imbas in its most pure form suddenly leap out of the Cauldron of Wisdom and land on your tongue. Several things happen at once. You immediately see every enlightened god, poet and hero who drank from this Cauldron and gained the powers of the Samildanach, the god who knows all and is good at everything. Your internal Cauldron emerges from your belly in music and fire, and your consciousness disappears in its blazing glory. Everything around you disappears, and you open your eyes in the world above. Light shines out from your face. You suddenly realize that you have been reborn as a radiant infant.

appendix- personal experiences

I've saved some of my most personal interpretations and experiences with the Cauldron text for this appendix, because I wanted to leave room for your Imbas to teach you different things from what my Imbas has taught me. So, think of the following as what modern pagans call UPG or "unverified personal gnosis"- material based solely on my own experience of Imbas Forosnai rather than being backed up by even the most speculative interpretation of historical evidence. Many of these things were experienced prior to my recent translation of the Cauldron text and "deep reading" of its contents, but I've been working with Imbas Forosnai for about twenty-five years.

Because this is a cthonic practice, you may have frightening dreams where you encounter the dead or the primal Chaos forces such as the Fomorians. These experiences can be very dark, very upsetting and very scary. However, you should welcome your encounters with such forces because they have the wisdom of the underworld to give. Be extremely cautious about making any deals with such entities when you encounter them in your dreams. If they offer to tell you something, just listen respectfully. If they try to harm you, call on Brighid for protection and her power will unfailingly disperse them.

You may encounter a force or power that feels like powerful electricity or intoxication coursing through your body. This is raw magical power- the Brig or the Imbas or the Tein Fesa. It can have a light, dark or neutral quality. If it has a dark quality, try to transform it into a light, joyful energy or learn how to work with the dark power without being overwhelmed by it.

Sometimes the power can manifest as a spiral. This may be a whirlpool on the ocean or a tornado on the land, or a spiraling ball of energy between your hands, or you may begin to spin around and around in the dream, or to float or rise up through the air in a spiraling movement. The spiral can move in the blessed clockwise direction or in the uncanny counterclockwise direction.

Because *coire* can mean either "cauldron" or "whirlpool" in Old Irish, I interpret this spiraling power as the power of the Cauldron, turning or "cooking" whatever it contains. This means the spiral energy has the power to transform things. If you are confronted by a dead or Fomorian entity, you can raise up this spiral power and use it to dissolve the spirit. However- and remembering to do this while dreaming is not easy- if you use the power to dissolve yourself instead, it can cause the entire structure of the dream to fall apart, activating your Cauldron of Wisdom.

Sometimes you can encounter gods or goddesses in dreams. Sometimes you will only realize you were talking to a god or goddess after you wake up.

Sometimes you might have a dream of a storm or a flood or a giant wave or a rushing torrent of water, often accompanied by an eerie glow that seems to suffuse everything in the dream. This kind of dream is usually so vivid and intense that it actually feels "more real" than regular daily life. If you recognize this torrent of water for what it is- the overflowing waters of the Well of Segais- you can choose to let it "rip you apart" as it did Boann, destroying the dream world. (If you don't recognize the waters in the dream, you'll just try to run away.)

When I remembered to allow the waters to tear me apart, everything in the dream disappeared and I had a sense of "breaking through" into an infinite field of limitless love, bliss, blazing light and perfect freedom. I still had a sense of existence as a distinct being within the field of light, but no body or other characteristics.

In a later dream-vision, I found myself in a group of faceless people standing on a rocky ridge that sloped downward toward a valley of utter darkness, a darkness as complete as in the depths of a cave. We were led by a faceless man with the gestures and mannerisms of a carnival barker. He was gesturing rather grandly for us to proceed down the slope into the valley of darkness, but we were all too terrified to do so because it was obvious the pitch blackness of the valley would swallow us up the moment we stepped past a certain point. Our guide's mannerisms did not inspire trust, but I reached down and picked up a handful of pebbles to test the reality of the scene in which I found myself. At this moment, I realized our guide was a psychopomp and we were in the land of death. Deciding to take a leap of faith, I raised my hands in prayer and walked downward into the dark. The result was exactly the same as the previous visions of blazing light except that the visual impression was of total darkness. I found myself soaring blissfully through perfect and absolutely limitless ecstatic joy.

I interpret these visions as the manifestation of the Cauldron of Wisdom and the turning of the Cauldron from the upside-down position onto its side. (If it had been upright, I probably would have had no sense of distinct identity.) I've had the same dream-vision on two or three occasions, but I have never gone further than that. When the Cauldron of Wisdom turns partially upright, it doesn't last long. Regular life pulls it back into the upside-down position.

Appendix- Invocation of the Graces: A Brigidine Sacred Text
Originally published on Patheos Agora, "Loop of Brighid"

1

Several versions of the "Invocation of the Graces" appear in the *Carmina Gadelica*, the massive collection of Gaelic prayers and charms collected and edited by folklorist Alexander Carmichael in the late nineteenth century. The "Invocation of the Graces" is a charm or blessing that was recited over young people in the Scottish Highlands to protect them from various potential threats while endowing them with a number of virtues or powers Carmichael's translation refers to as "graces."

The version of the "Invocation of the Graces" that appears in Volume I of the *Carmina Gadelica* only mentions Brighid in passing as one of several female powers who provide the graces. However, the versions given in Volume III name Brighid as the creator of the charm:

The grace placed by Brigit,
Maiden of graces,
In the daughter of the king,
Gile-Mhin the beauteous.

If the charm was originally spoken by Brighid as a blessing on Gile-Mhin, then we can think of the entire charm as the words of Brighid. When you read the words of the "Invocation" in your mind, you can think of them as being spoken by Brighid Herself.

There was more than one version of the "Invocation of the Graces," and Carmichael is thought to have embellished his sources to some extent to produce a coherent version out of fragmentary survivals from the oral tradition. As such, there is really no definitive text of the original charm, so we will be examining selected verses from more than one version. The verses we will be discussing in this series are as follows:

I bathe thy palms
In showers of wine,
In the lustral fire,
In the seven elements,
In the juice of the rasps,
In the milk of honey,
And I place the nine pure choice graces
In thy fair fond face,
The grace of form,
The grace of voice,
The grace of fortune,
The grace of goodness,
The grace of wisdom,
The grace of charity,
The grace of choice maidenliness,
The grace of whole-souled loveliness,
The grace of goodly speech.

Dark is yonder town,
Dark are those therein,
Thou art the brown swan,
Going in among them.
Their hearts are under thy control,
Their tongues are beneath thy sole,
Nor will they ever utter a word
To give thee offense.

A shade art thou in the heat,
A shelter art thou in the cold,
Eyes art thou to the blind,
A staff art thou to the pilgrim,
An island art thou at sea,

A fortress art thou on land,
A well art thou in the desert,
Health art thou to the ailing.

Thine is the skill of the Fairy Woman,
Thine is the virtue of Bride the calm,
Thine is the faith of Mary the mild,
Thine is the tact of the woman of Greece,
Thine is the beauty of Emir the lovely,
Thine is the tenderness of Darthula delightful,
Thine is the courage of Maebh the strong,
Thine is the charm of Binne-bheul.

Thou art the joy of all joyous things,
Thou art the light of the beam of the sun,
Thou art the door of the chief of hospitality,
Thou art the surpassing star of guidance,
Thou art the step of the deer of the hill,
Thou art the step of the steed of the plain,
Thou art the grace of the swan of swimming,
Thou art the loveliness of all lovely desires.

Grace upwards over thee,
Grace downwards over thee,
Grace of graces without gainsaying.

Grace of form,
Grace of fortune,
Grace of voice,
Excellence of men.
Excellence of women,
Excellence of lover.
Excellence of sons and of daughters be thine.

Excellence of corn,
Excellence of drink,

Excellence of music,
Excellence of guiding,
Excellence of sea and land be thine.

Excellence of sitting.
Excellence of journeying,
Excellence of cattle,
Excellence of churning.

Excellence of curds and butter be thine.
Excellence of the swan of the fountain,
Excellence of sheep and of wool.
Excellence of kids and of goats.
Lasting excellence by day and night be thine.

Grace of the love of the skies be thine,
Grace of the love of the stars be thine,
Grace of the love of the moon be thine,
Grace of the love of the sun be thine.

The word translated as "excellence" in these verses is actually *buadh*, the same word translated as "graces." So there are clearly far more than nine of them! In this series of articles, I will go through the "Invocation of the Graces" verse by verse, analyzing it to discover what it has to teach us about Brigidine devotion, virtue ethics and spirituality.

2

According to Carmichael, the "Invocation" was spoken over boys and girls in some districts and over young men and women in others. Although the feeling and tone of the "Invocation" are feminine, it was never understood as being "just for girls."

This point is particularly interesting in that the purpose of the charm is to endow the recipient with specific powers and virtues.

The "Invocation" is not only a piece of folk magic but a commentary on virtue ethics. Many systems of virtue ethics seem to come from a very masculine perspective. For instance, the "nine noble virtues" of Asatru are courage, truth, honor, fidelity, discipline, hospitality, industriousness, self-reliance and perseverance. These are not portrayed as being "just for men," but their relationship to the masculine warrior ethos of the Icelandic sagas is clear. As a discussion of "virtue ethics" based on a distinctly feminine perspective, the "Invocation of the Graces" provides an interesting contrast to the nine noble virtues.

Although I will continue to use the title "Invocation of the Graces" because it is so widely known, the Gaelic word translated as "graces" does not have the same connotations as the English word. *Buadh* in Gaelic doesn't really mean "graces" at all. According to the Gaelic dictionary *Am Faclair Beag*, it actually means an attribute, faculty, talent or virtue. The closely related word *buaidh* means success, conquest, victory, impact, influence, mastery or predominance.

Rather than "Invocation of the Graces," *Ora nam Buadh* could more accurately be translated as "Song of the Virtues," with the understanding that the virtues in this case imply victory and success in life. In ancient times, the word *buadh* referred to the special powers or excellences of great heroes like Cuchulain, although these powers were understood to derive from the goddesses of the pre-Christian religion. According to the *Dindsenchas*, the goddess Macha (one of the three Morrigans) "diffused all excellences" and was the "sun of womankind."

So, if the *buaidh* or "graces" are really virtues, powers or excellences traditionally believed to be granted by goddesses with solar connections like Brighid and Macha, then the "Invocation of the Graces" should be understood as the words of power with which Brighid grants the graces to Her devotees- in other words, a Brigidine sacred text.

In the first verse, Brighid says:

*I bathe thy palms
In showers of wine,
In the lustral fire,
In the seven elements,
In the juice of the rasps,
In the milk of honey,
And I place the nine pure choice graces
In thy fair fond face...*

The first thing that stands out about this verse is that it describes a ritual purification through bathing. As P. Sufenus Virius Lupus pointed out in his article "The Hidden Imbolc," this concept is central to the oldest lore of Brighid's festival, which involves a ritual bath using milk or butter to purify young warriors or reivers and reintegrate them into the community.

Carmichael tells us that the "Invocation" was used to bless young men and women, and expresses the opinion that it was originally composed for a young woman on her wedding day. What if it was actually composed for a young man going on or returning from his first raid against an enemy clan? Some versions of the "Invocation" protect the recipient from being harmed by swords, spears and other weapons. This is much more likely to be a concern for a young reiver than a young bride. Considering that the prayer was actually used to bless both boys and girls, it was probably phrased so as to apply to both.

The phrase Carmichael renders as "showers of wine" is *frasa fiona*. A *fras* is a rain shower or scattering of water, so a "shower of wine" is probably a sprinkling of wine over the palms.

The phrase Carmichael translates as "lustral flame" is *liu nan lasa*, which literally means "water of the fire." Fiery water is a very ancient concept in Indo-European religions, and closely associated with the goddess Brighid and related deities. The well of wisdom at the roots of the World Tree is supposed to be filled with this fiery water.

The "seven elements" are the *duilean* of Gaelic lore, of which both the world and each individual human being are made. This is also an ancient Indo-European concept. Numerous different versions of the *duilean* exist. The "Body of Adam" text includes earth (flesh), water (blood), sun (face or eyes), clouds (mind), wind (breath), stones (bones) and spirit. However, the phrase used here is *seachd siona*, a different version of the seven elements listed by *Am Faclair Beag* as fire, air, earth, water, ice, wind and lightning.

The phrase Carmichael translates as "juice of the rasps" is *subh-craobh*. This refers to a raspberry bush or any other bush that produces wild berries. In the folktale of "Great Brid of the Horses," Brid demands an offering of blackberries in winter. Wild berry juice or wine could therefore be seen as a symbol of Brighid.

Carmichael's "milk of honey" is *bainne meala*, literally "honey milk." Giraldus Cambrensis, in describing the Awenyddion or Welsh seers, has this to say:

These gifts are usually conferred upon them in dreams: some seem to have sweet milk or honey poured on their lips...

The Welsh word *awen* refers to the power of inspiration granted by the muse Cerridwen to the Welsh bards. It is equivalent to the Irish *imbas*.

So, this first verse of the "Invocation" describes a purification ritual in which Brighid washes the recipient's palms and face with some kind of wine or mead made of berry juice, milk and honey.

This drink is the "fiery water" of the well of wisdom, containing the powers of the seven primordial elements and the *imbas* of the goddess.

3

After the description of the ritual bath with the wine of *imbas*, the "Invocation" goes on to list the nine "graces" or virtues:

The grace of form,
The grace of voice,
The grace of fortune,
The grace of goodness,
The grace of wisdom,
The grace of charity,
The grace of choice maidenliness,
The grace of whole-souled loveliness,
The grace of goodly speech.

The word Carmichael translates as "form" is *cruth*, which Gaelic dictionary *Am Faclair Beag* defines as form, figure, shape, countenance, personal appearance or facial expression.

The word Carmichael translates as "voice" is *guth*, which *Am Faclair Beag* defines as either the voice or a word or the mention of a thing.

The word Carmichael translates as "fortune" is *rath*, which *Am Faclair Beag* defines as "good fortune."

The word Carmichael translates as "goodness" is *math,* which *Am Faclair Beag* defines as goodness, profit, advantage or prosperity.

The word Carmichael translates as "wisdom" is *cnoc*, which *Am Faclair Beag* defines as "hill." However, the Gaelic dictionary at Glosbe.com notes that *cnoc* can also mean wisdom as Carmichael says. This may be a reference to the Gaelic belief that special skills or excellences such as the *buaidh* derived from the power of the dead or the fairies in their hollow hills. Gaelic scholar Michael Newton describes this concept in detail in his essay <u>*Bha mi 's a chnoc: Creativity in Scottish Gaelic Tradition*</u>, in which the phrase *bha mi 's a chnoc* literally means "I was in the hill".

The word Carmichael translates as "charity" is *bochd*, which *Am Faclair Beag* defines as poverty, difficulty or illness. It isn't easy to see how this could qualify as a *buadh*, as the word has no positive connotations in Gaelic. Carmichael might have assumed that the word must originally have been something else, but my guess would be that *buaidh bochd* is supposed to mean "victory over poverty."

The phrase Carmichael translates as "choice maidenliness" is *rogha finne*. According to *Am Faclair Beag*, the word *rogha* means "the best of" or "the choice of" and *finne* means a maiden, a beautiful woman, whiteness or fairness. So the phrase could be expressed as "choice womanhood".

The phrase Carmichael translates as "whole-souled loveliness" is *fior eireachdais*. According to *Am Faclair Beag*, the word *fior* means true, genuine or pure and *eireachdais* means beauty or handsomeness. *Fior* can also mean "fire."

The phrase Carmichael translates as "goodly speech" is *deagh labhraidh*. According to *Am Faclair Beag*, the word *deagh* means "good" and *labhraidh* means "diction."

At first glance, this list might seem a lot more appropriate for a young woman than a young man, as the graces in question would be seen in our culture as entirely feminine: a beautiful face and figure, a charming voice, true elegance even in poverty. However, young Highlanders of the warrior class were expected to display a graceful, elegant bearing. The sons of clan chieftains studied dancing and swordsmanship at the same schools, so grace and beauty were not necessarily seen as being un-masculine.

Another clue that this list of nine graces is not merely intended to make the recipient a socially acceptable young lady is that the very next verse is about achieving complete domination over all your enemies:

Dark is yonder town,
Dark are those therein,
Thou art the brown swan,
Going in among them.
Their hearts are under thy control,
Their tongues are beneath thy sole,
Nor will they ever utter a word
To give thee offense.

According to Carmichael, "brown swan" is a Gaelic euphemism for a young girl, with "white swan" indicating an older one. Another prayer in the Carmina Gadelica uses very similar imagery to pray for justice:

God, I am bathing my face
In the nine rays of the sun,
As Mary bathed her Son
In generous milk fermented.

Sweetness be in my face,
Riches be in my countenance,
Comb-honey be in my tongue,
My breath as the incense.

Black is yonder house,
Blacker men therein;
I am the white swan,
Queen over them.

I will go in the name of God,
In likeness of deer, in likeness of horse,
In likeness of serpent, in likeness of king,
More victorious am I than all persons.

Although this prayer for justice mentions Mary rather than Brighid, the imagery of bathing in sunlight and milk connects it to Brighid and to the "Invocation of the Graces." The power of the "Invocation of the Graces" to grant victory over one's enemies should not be seen as something given in addition to the feminine charms listed in the first verse, but because of them. The word *buaidh*, after all, means "victory."

When Brighid bathes your palms and cheeks in Her "lustral fire," in Her milk and sunlight, in Her honey and wine, She not only grants you Her beauty and elegance but makes you "more victorious than all persons."

4

For some unknown reason, the remaining blessings and *buaidh* in the "Invocation" are generally grouped into lists of eight rather than nine. The first set of eight blessings reads as follows:

A shade art thou in the heat,
A shelter art thou in the cold,
Eyes art thou to the blind,
A staff art thou to the pilgrim,
An island art thou at sea,
A fortress art thou on land,
A well art thou in the desert,
Health art thou to the ailing.

This is the first section of the "Invocation" that could be described as an ethical guideline. The recipient of the charm has been rendered powerful enough to overcome all enemies, but is now expected to use that power in compassionate service.

All eight of these "ethical empowerments" express essentially the same concept: to relieve the suffering of others by providing comfort, shelter, guidance, support, sanctuary, protection, refreshment or healing. Only one of the eight uses martial imagery. The phrase "a fortress art thou on land" implies that you will fight if necessary to protect an endangered person just like a warrior defending a besieged fortress. This type of fight is defensive and protective in nature, not aggressive or predatory.

The next verse in the Invocation, which calls on eight feminine powers to grant eight ethical virtues, also includes one martial reference:

Thine is the skill of the Fairy Woman,
Thine is the virtue of Bride the calm,
Thine is the faith of Mary the mild,
Thine is the tact of the woman of Greece,
Thine is the beauty of Emir the lovely,
Thine is the tenderness of Darthula delightful,
Thine is the courage of Maebh the strong,
Thine is the charm of Binne-bheul.

The word Carmichael translates as "skill" is *gleus*, which the Gaelic dictionary *Am Faclair Beag* defines as a condition, a state of being, a mood or humor, the workings of a machine, or a musical key. This is clearly a word that has no precise translation into English, but it conveys the idea of an inner order or structure.

The word Carmichael translates as "virtue" is *beus*, which *Am Faclair Beag* defines as moral virtue or conduct. The word Carmichael defines as "calm" is *bithe*. According to *Am Faclair Beag*, this can mean "peaceful" or "tranquil." It can also mean "female."

The word Carmichael translates as "faith" is *creud*, which *Am Faclair Beag* defines as a creed or belief. Religions are usually referred to as "creeds" in Gaelic, as in the phrase "the creed of the yellow stick" as a euphemism for Protestantism. The word Carmichael translates as "mild" is *mine*, which *Am Faclair Beag* defines as "mild" or "gentle."

The word Carmichael translates as "tact" is *gniomh*, which *Am Faclair Beag* does not define as "tact" but as an action, deed or task. As such, it is difficult to know what virtue is being granted here without knowing what the task of the "woman of Greece" was. William Sharp (generally a questionable source) suggests that this line refers to Helen of Troy. That is not implausible, since the legend of Helen was known to the Gaels although Helen of Troy was not exactly famed for her tact. If "the deed of Helen of Troy" is really what was meant here, it might have referred to her famous seductiveness.

The word Carmichael translates as "beauty" is *sgeimh*, which *Am Faclair Beag* defines as elegance. Emir, of course, was the wife of the great Irish hero Cuchulain.

The word Carmichael translates as "tenderness" is *mein,* which *Am Faclair Beag* does not give a definition for, although *mèinneach* is defined as mercy, pity, discreetness or fondness. Carmichael's "Darthula" (a Victorian-era name meaning "daughter of heaven") is actually Dearshul in the Gaelic. Sharp suggests this is a corruption of Deirdre, tragic heroine of "The Sons of Uisneach."

The word Carmichael translates as "courage" is *mean*, presumably short for *meanmna,* which *Am Faclair Beag* defines as courage, boldness, spirit, pride or joy. "The courage of Maebh the strong" is the bold, spirited, joyful or even reckless courage of Queen Maebh of the Tain, cattle-raider par excellence, who warred against Cuchulain. Unlike the phrase "a fortress art thou on land," this one is aggressive- the most "heathen" of the graces!

The word Carmichael translates as "charm" is *taladh*, which *Am Faclair Beag* defines as the act of enticing, alluring, taming, soothing, domesticating, caressing or hushing. The range of meanings can cover everything from charming a potential romantic partner to calming a wild horse to singing a lullaby to a crying baby. *Binne-bheul* is "sweet-mouth." Sharp, interpreting the phrase as "honey-mouth," suggests that it refers to the Gaelic god Angus. However, *Am Faclair Beag* specifically mentions that the sweetness of *binne* is not a flavor or a smell, but something harmonious or musical. Also, it would be a little odd for the "Invocation" to list seven female powers and one male power, so it seems more likely to refer to a woman from Gaelic lore.

5

The ambiguity of some of the Gaelic words and phrases in the "Invocation of the Graces" makes it difficult to say exactly what virtues Brighid is supposed to be granting to the recipient of the charm. Some of Carmichael's translation choices seem to skew towards a Victorian conception of feminine virtue.

The three most difficult phrases in the list are *gleus na Mnatha Sithe* or "skill of the Fairy Woman," *gniomh na mnatha Grég* or "tact of the woman of Greece" and *mein na Dearshul agha* or "tenderness of Darthula delightful."

All of the eight virtues granted by the eight feminine powers seem to refer to specific incidents in Gaelic oral tradition, even if we cannot always tell which story is being referred to. To come up with a set of eight virtues we can actually work with, we need to consider all the implications of each line in the original Gaelic.

"Skill of the Fairy Woman" is not a bad translation of *gleus na*

Mnatha Sithe considering the difficulty of translating *gleus*. However, simplifying the concept down to "skill" would be highly distorting. The idea is not skill in a generalized sense, but a state of being like that of a fairy woman. In Gaelic tradition, fairy women are powerful, dangerous, seductive, capable of granting poetic inspiration and eternal life in Tir na n-Og, but equally capable of draining away a man's life-force or changing into a raven and eating the flesh of the fallen on the battlefield. They are perilous entities to have anything to do with- not that that ever stops anyone!

An inner state like that of a fairy woman could possibly be rendered in English as "enchantment"- as long as we bear in mind the darker implications of that word.

Of course, the phrase "fairy woman" carries very different connotations in English than in Gaelic. It would probably be less distorting to translate *Mnatha Sithe* as "woman of the otherworld" rather than "fairy woman."

As we have seen, *"gniomh na mnatha Grég"* is probably not "tact of the woman of Greece," since *gniomh* means a deed or a task. It's not impossible that the line refers to Helen of Troy as Sharp suggests, but it could just as easily refer to any number of Gaelic folktales where the hero visits a fantastic imaginary version of Greece. It is probably best to simply translate this word as "deed," as the doing of heroic deeds fits both the sense of the original and the concept of a list of virtues.

The phrase *"mein na Dearshul agha"* can only mean "tenderness of Darthula delightful" if we interpret *mein* as mercy or pity, but this seems unlikely. An analysis of Gaelic compounds containing *mèin* or *mein* suggests that the word should be translated as temperament or character. For instance, *ain-mèin* is pride, haughtiness or arrogance according to *am Faclair Beag* while *gabh ain-mèin* means to become enraged and *ainmein* means fury or rage. *Ain* is a negative prefix in Gaelic, so *ain-mèin* is the state of losing your *mèin*. It seems similar to the concept of "losing your temper" in English.

Bearing in mind the difficulties of translating these phrases with any confidence, I suggest that this verse of the "Invocation" might be rendered as follows:

Thine is the enchantment of the woman of the otherworld,
Thine is the virtue of Bride the calm,
Thine is the faith of Mary the mild,
Thine is the deed of the woman of Greece,
Thine is the elegance of Emir the lovely,
Thine is the character of Dearshul delightful,
Thine is the boldness of Maebh the strong,
Thine is the charm of the Melodious Mouth.

So, our list of eight virtues is either skill, virtue, faith, tact, beauty, tenderness, courage and charm (as Carmichael would have it) or the following rather different list:

1- enchantment
2- virtue
3- faith
4- deeds
5- elegance
6- character
7- boldness
8- charm

The second list presents a rather different portrait of both virtue and femininity than what emerges from Carmichael's translation.

6

The next verse in the "Invocation of the Graces" uses primarily images drawn from the natural world to convey another set of eight blessings:

Thou art the joy of all joyous things,
Thou art the light of the beam of the sun,
Thou art the door of the chief of hospitality,
Thou art the surpassing star of guidance,
Thou art the step of the deer of the hill,
Thou art the step of the steed of the plain,
Thou art the grace of the swan of swimming,
Thou art the loveliness of all lovely desires.

Carmichael's translation of these phrases is fairly literal for the most part. The phrase Carmichael translates as "the joy of all joyous things" is *"sonas gach ni eibhinn,"* which could be "happiness of every cheerful thing" or "bliss of every funny thing" according to the Gaelic dictionary *Am Faclair Beag*. The word *eibhinn* generally means something odd, funny or joyful.

"The light of the beam of the sun" brings to mind the solar associations of Brighid, which is not surprising because She is supposed to be the one speaking the charm.

"The door of the chief of hospitality" refers to the Gaelic custom of keeping open house. Chiefs and kings would leave their doors open at all times to display their extravagant generosity and hospitality, and any person could come in and receive food and drink free of charge. No chief would have been considered a genuine chief if he failed to uphold this custom. St. Brighid of Kildare was renowned for her generosity, especially with the wealth of the rich and powerful men who owned her when she was a slave!

"The surpassing star of guidance" seems like a reference to the symbolism of Imbolc. The *reul-iuil Bride* or "guiding star of Brighid" is a star-shaped ornament attached above the heart on the Brighid doll families would make at Imbolc.

"The step of the deer of the hill" implies a light-footed, graceful quality, while "the step of the steed of the plain" implies a proud, domineering quality. The phrase Carmichael translates as "the step of the steed of the plain" is *"ceum steud nam blaru."* A *"blàr"* is a field or a plain, but the word is often used in the names of Gaelic battlefields, as in the famous clan fight of *Blàr na Pàirce*. *Am Faclair Beag* lists "battlefield" as one of the definitions of the word.

In the phrase "the grace of the swan of the swimming," the word Carmichael translates as "grace" is *seimh,* which *Am Faclair Beag* defines as calmness, gentleness, mildness or kindness.

In the phrase "the loveliness of all lovely desires," the word Carmichael translates as "loveliness" is *ailleagan,* which *Am Faclair Beag* defines as a little jewel or treasure, noting that the word is used as an endearment for young people. The word Carmichael translates as "all lovely desires" is *rùn.* This interesting word is etymologically related to the Norse "rune" but it means a mystery or a secret. When used in phrases such as *mo rùn* ("my love") it means "love." So this phrase could be rendered as "thou art the little jewel of the mystery of love."

In the version of "Invocation of the Graces" that appears in the first volume of the Carmina Gadelica, this verse is the last verse that does not rely heavily on Christian concepts and images. In fact, by invoking some of Brighid's elemental powers of sunlight and starlight, animal qualities like those of deers, steeds and swans and the ancient Celtic ideology of hospitality, this verse could be considered somewhat "pagan." The rest of the verses in this version concentrate on God and the saints, so we'll be examining a different version of the "Invocation" next time.

7

Carmichael's sources in the Gaelic community collected more than one version of the "Invocation of the Graces," some of which have a different tone than the more familiar version. Carmina Gadelica #279 focuses on protecting the recipient of the charm from various weapons, raising the possibility that this was the version of the "Invocation" spoken over young men while the version in Volume 1 (Carmina Gadelica #3) was spoken over young women. Carmichael doesn't actually say this, though- he says that #3 was spoken over both sexes.

The following verses are from #278:

Grace upwards over thee,
Grace downwards over thee,
Grace of graces without gainsaying.

Grace of form,
Grace of fortune,
Grace of voice,
Excellence of men.
Excellence of women,
Excellence of lover.
Excellence of sons and of daughters be thine.

Note that three of the "graces" are the same as in #3- the graces of form, fortune and voice. In general, though, this version of the "Invocation" concentrates more on conferring practical benefits in life: protection from head to toes, a good mate or lover, great kids. The same theme is continued in the next few verses:

Excellence of corn,
Excellence of drink,
Excellence of music,
Excellence of guiding,
Excellence of sea and land be thine.

Excellence of sitting.
Excellence of journeying,
Excellence of cattle,
Excellence of churning.

Excellence of curds and butter be thine.
Excellence of the swan of the fountain,
Excellence of sheep and of wool.
Excellence of kids and of goats.
Lasting excellence by day and night be thine.

In these verses, Brighid confers the blessings of good food and drink, music, a thriving goat and sheep farm and abundant dairy products. Then the last verse suddenly gets poetic:

Grace of the love of the skies be thine,
Grace of the love of the stars be thine,
Grace of the love of the moon be thine,
Grace of the love of the sun be thine.

The word Carmichael translates as "love" in these verses is *rùn*. As we have seen, *rùn* means both "love" and "mystery," so these lines could just as easily be rendered as follows:

Grace of the mystery of the skies be thine,
Grace of the mystery of the stars be thine,
Grace of the mystery of the moon be thine,
Grace of the mystery of the sun be thine.

The ancient Gaels swore oaths on the sun, moon and stars. Modern devotees of Brighid sometimes think of Her as not only a sun goddess but a goddess of all the suns (the stars) and of the moon (since its light is reflected sunlight). These ideas are dependent on scientific facts unknown the ancient Gaels, but could find some support in these lines since they are supposed to be spoken by Brighid Herself. You could say that Brighid is able to convey the powers of the sun, moon and stars because they are Her own powers. This interpretation receives additional support from the Imbolc custom of making pictures of the sun, moon and stars.

8

Having gone through a number of verses from the "Invocation of the Graces" line by line, I would now like to present a new translation of those same verses that incorporates some of the connotations Carmichael left out of his translation. The extent to which Carmichael contributed his own material to the original folklore cannot be known- some people think he might have added a line or two, while others think he pretty much wrote the "Invocation" himself- so I'm giving my translation a new title to emphasize the fact that any translation is essentially an original work.

Translating *buaidh* as "graces" emphasizes the Victorian ideal of femininity. That emphasis is much less present in the Gaelic version, which still comes across as feminine but in a much less Victorian way. The word is more accurately translated as "power" or "virtue," but with a root meaning of "victory." Throughout my version of the charm, I translate *buaidh* as "virtue" except in the last verse where I have translated it as "power." All verses except the last verse are from Carmina Gadelica #3; the final verse is from Carmina Gadelica #278, which is another version of the same charm.

I have kept Carmichael's use of "thee" and "thine" because it reflects the Gaelic distinction between *tu* and *sibh*. "You" or *"sibh"* is plural or formal, while "thee" or *"tu"* is singular or informal. Prayers traditionally use "thee" not to sound pseudo-archaic but to emphasize intimacy with the divine.

Song of the Virtues

*I bathe thy palms
In showers of wine,
In the fiery water,
In the seven elements,
In the juice of berries,
In the honey milk,
And I place the nine pure choice virtues
In thy fair fond face:*

*Virtue of form,
Virtue of voice,
Virtue of fortune,
Virtue of goodness,
Virtue of wisdom,
Virtue over poverty,
Virtue of choice womanhood,
Virtue of true beauty,
Virtue of good speech.*

*Dark is yonder town,
Dark are those therein,
Thou art the brown swan,
Going in among them.
Their hearts are under thy control,
Their tongues are beneath thy sole,
Nor will they ever utter a word
To give thee offense.*

*A shade art thou in the heat,
A shelter art thou in the cold,
Eyes art thou to the blind,
A staff art thou to the pilgrim,
An island art thou at sea,
A fortress art thou on land,*

A well art thou in the desert,
Health art thou to the ailing.

Thine is the enchantment of the woman of the otherworld,
Thine is the virtue of Bride the calm,
Thine is the faith of Mary the mild,
Thine is the deed of the woman of Greece,
Thine is the elegance of Emir the lovely,
Thine is the character of Dearshul delightful,
Thine is the boldness of Maebh the strong,
Thine is the charm of the Melodious Mouth.

Thou art the joy of all joyous things,
Thou art the light of the beam of the sun,
Thou art the door of the chief of hospitality,
Thou art the surpassing star of guidance,
Thou art the step of the deer of the hill,
Thou art the step of the steed of the battlefield,
Thou art the virtue of the swan of swimming,
Thou art the little jewel of the mystery of love.

Power of the mystery of the skies be thine,
Power of the mystery of the stars be thine,
Power of the mystery of the moon be thine,
Power of the mystery of the sun be thine.

9

To conclude this discussion of the "Invocation of the Graces," I'd like to present an outline of the charm and the virtues and powers it grants.

In the first verse, Brighid bathes the recipient's palms and face in a special drink of "fiery water" made of milk mixed with berry wine and honey.

In the second verse, the fiery water grants nine virtues or powers: the virtue of form, voice, fortune, goodness and wisdom, victory over poverty, the virtue of choice womanhood, the virtue of true beauty, and the virtue of good speech.

In the third verse, the fiery water grants the ability to dominate all enemies, rendering them silent and submissive.

In the fourth verse, the fiery water grants eight ethical empowerments, giving the recipient of the charm the ability to offer comfort, shelter, guidance, support, sanctuary, protection, refreshment and healing to those who need it.

In the fifth verse, the fiery water grants the qualities of eight feminine powers: enchantment, virtue, faith, deeds, elegance, character, boldness and charm.

In the sixth verse, the fiery water grants powers and virtues drawn mostly but not exclusively from the natural world. These virtues are a bit more abstract, but include qualities such as good humor, sunniness, hospitality, a sense of direction, light-footedness, high-spiritedness, elegant dignity and love.

Some versions of the charm include verses granting a number of worldly benefits such as a good lover or plenty of nourishing food. Others include verses granting protection from weapons, malicious spirits and other dangers. Some include a verse granting the powers of celestial bodies such as the sun, moon and stars.

As mentioned previously, the "graces" could be seen as a system of virtue ethics based on an idealized femininity, in contrast to the idealized masculinity of heathenism's "nine noble virtues." By "femininity" and "masculinity" I don't mean the biology of having a female or male body, and neither did the Highlanders who used this charm in the past- otherwise they wouldn't have recited it over both boys and girls. Instead, I'm using "femininity" to refer to a certain type of energy, the energy of Brighid. I take it for granted that feminine and masculine energies are accessible in some degree to every person regardless of biological sex. The "nine noble virtues" are equally virtuous for both men and women but they express a more "masculine" energy. Similarly, the nine "victories" of this charm are equally victorious for both women and men, but they express a more "feminine" energy.

By "femininity" I also don't mean a set of stereotyped expectations of passive or proper behavior. The charm grants the courage of Maebh, after all, and Maebh was anything but passive or proper. By including Maebh in the list of feminine powers, the charm values the courage and even the reckless ferocity of the warrior- but it does so in balance and proportion with other virtues that emphasize compassion, beauty and a gentle spirit.

The feminine energy of the "Invocation of the Graces" is the power of Brighid in action in the world. To understand this power and to live in imitation of it is to experience victory, enabling you to do good in the world by serving others with compassion and to defeat evil by rendering it silent and powerless. Just as devoted Christians seek to live in imitation of Christ as revealed to them in the Gospel story, devotees of Brighid can live in imitation of Her graces, as revealed in this Gaelic charm.

appendix- sorrows and joys

In case you're curious about the notion of modern poetry being produced from the Cauldron's list of joys and sorrows, here are a few examples.

Stormrider- a poem written in memory of my father David Douglas Thompson, who passed away in 2006 while competing in the Sunfish World Championships. This poem expresses the sorrow of longing for absent loved ones.

1

You cast a heavy shadow. Years will pass
Yet none who knew will ever lose the sight
Of one bright, piercing eye. You walked the world
In such a wild and vivid way, your mark
As potent as a rune on all you touched.
The rider of a winter storm, the wolf
Of wind and water and the wizard-king
Of salt and spray, an alchemist of song,
Who turned the darkness seen at Jacob's Pond
To fearsome music, and the saddest plans
The gods prepared for madmen into notes
Of such weird beauty that they seem to ring
Between the moments of this floating life
In haunted echoes. Not for you the pale,
Transparent destinies of modern man:
The doubts, the smallness and the final fall
From *very little* into *not at all.*
Your failures and your victories were large.
In everything you did you waged a long,
Determined bout with heaven, till the dawn
Lit both of you to laughter. Now you're gone.
An old, unbeaten rebel, taken back
To somewhere far away, beyond our dreams.
But every now and then it almost seems
That I can hear your voice. And what it says
Is, "Hold the course. The fight is far from done."

2

So, Captain, what is next? Do ghosts advise?
I've waged a war myself, these many years.

And yet, before you left us, you'd been cleansed
And purified by suffering so harsh
It almost broke you, into something new-
A calmer man, if never quite content.
You spent your last year pondering the past,
The things that made you and the things you made.
With pipe in mouth you watched the seasons change
While, flickering behind your eyes, the tales
Of lore and legend leaped like dancing sparks.
You loved to tell those stories! And, in all,
You featured as the hero. But your voice
Wove such a spell of magic round the words
That legend came to life for us. And now,
Tall tales and all, you've fallen into sleep.
I never wept except for that first night.
It didn't seem correct, somehow. I knew
You left this world as you'd have wanted to,
The ocean wind behind you and the spray
Blown cold against your face, the dark green sea
In all its ancient fury close beside,
And one task only- race, and try to win.
You didn't quite have long enough. But then,
There's no one here who does or ever will.
And every day your shadow knows me still.

3

Yes, I was scared of you. That's true enough.
You had a madness deep behind your eyes,
That blazed sometimes, and kindled, deep in me,
A madness of my own. Your legacy
Is complicated and its roots are dim,
And knotted up as tight as tangled hair.
I look back on these deeds of mine and find
Much sorrow and my own dark share of shame,
And here and there a little quiet pride.
Were you the same? And did you face the night
With sick self-loathing for the things *you'd* done,
Or did you never dare to hear that voice?
It's not my wish to judge you. All your life
You struggled with the darkness, as have I.
I know the language of the night too well
To fail to recognize its mark in you,

And recognition is forgiveness. Still,
My task, I think, is this- to give my sons
The best of you and leave those things behind
That harmed us both. In this, I'll honor you.

4

Good blades will bend, yet still come back to true,
And hold the keenest edge. To forge a sword,
White heat is needed. So you forged my life,
And poured your lore into the blue-black steel
Of what I am. Now, dip me in a stream
And leaves will part against my sharpened edge.
God willing, my own children will be blades
As sharp as I am, but will have the skill
Of teaching leaves to turn aside, unharmed.
I'll hold the ground you conquered and move on
To claim new lands as well. I owe you that.
You climbed up from the pit to make a life
Worth singing of, a story to be told.
And if I tell of darkness with the light,
My Captain, please remember, Truth is One
And undivided and I cannot sing
A portion of the truth; there's no such thing.

5

So here I stand before the salt-blue sea,
My eyes averted from the open sky.
The breeze is cold, and breakers crash and roar,
While birds cry lonely omens. Here it comes.
I face the task you faced with me, and hope
That I'm equipped to do it. But I know
The hawk-like strength of all our kin is mine,
And all that's left is just to face my task
With bold, high spirit and with love's command.
And I will tell my children, so they'll know-
Their father's father was the kind of man
Who comes into this world, not every day
But once in many years. A wolf of wind
And ocean wave, a wizard of the sea,
An alchemist of music and a man
Who fought and didn't cease his fight until

The ocean waves closed over, cold and still.
And I will tell them also, what is true-
The core of what they see in me is you.

Your Secret History- a poem to express the sorrow of heartbreak after loss of love.

1
A red petal, placed on the space between
Your breasts, would taste tart as a mulberry
From the salt rhythms of your beating chest.

Pressed up against the soft skin of your wet
Stomach, I have yet to uncover the
Inexpressible redness of your night

Sky; and I have not yet discovered why
There is also a mask-like mystery
Moving between us in your living breath,

Whose eyes are like a glass marble, whose skies
Are speckled with histories of old storms
Like the skies of Jupiter. Like your eyes.

I have not yet uncovered your secret
History. There is a taste to your touch-
You are not quite like grape. There is much more.

2
The clouds wonder. Blue shapes ride the night
Sky. And as you light the holy incense,
Something slowly wanders by. Attracted by

The gleam in your eye or by the lovely
Severity with which you approach your
Task, divine monsters without form dissolve

Into silt at the bottom of your glass.
And after you have offered a prayer to
The wine-god, and born his blood as a mark

Below your lip, and when your skin is flushed
With his internal dancing, and when your

Heart begins to skip; then the silt of those

Divine monsters will drip like candlewax
As you begin your task. But I will be
More silent than the mask.

3
The clouds wonder. Echoes shudder in the
Sky. And in the not-too-distant future,
I might slowly wander by. Drawn closer by

The gleam in your eye or by the lovely
Severity with which you forget the
Past, I might appear in silt to haunt you

Or in the blank lines of a mask. And when
You have offered yourself to the wine-god,
And born his dancing as a mark below

Your chest, I might remind you of the
Red petal that I once placed between your
Breasts. I might remind you of your wet stomach,

And of the redness of your night sky.
But I will not discern these answers. I
Will not discover why.

4
There will be no mask-like mystery
To move between us in your living breath.
And if anything is a glass marble,

That is an eye with nothing left. So your
Skies will retain the mystery of
Old Jupiter's forgotten storms. But as

For my strange disappearance, I will take
On other forms. I couldn't break your code—
I struggled, I fought the watchers of the

Nighttime sun. I unraveled harsh equations,
But the lights went when I'd won. Now I am
Bathed in night's own water, strangely purified, but lost.

I am your intimation of a ghost.

Culdee- This poem was written from the perspective of an early Irish monk living as a hermit on a remote island, to express the sorrow of self-denial for the sake of the divine.

1

I found my private desert here. No sound
Of idle, empty talk. No talk at all.
I hear the moaning ocean, and the call
Of simple, greedy gulls. This patch of ground
Is void of any human thoughts but mine.
My chest is nearly empty, so that You
Can fill me absolutely. I am through
With all the chatter and the wasted time.
I spend my time in silent prayer. And I
Contain Your ocean and Your endless sky.

2

The ocean moans again. The gulls reply,
And I am on my knees. My floor is bare,
My walls are made of rocks I found. I stare
At nothing but Your face. And in my eye
The sufferings You paid for me are clear.
I hear the crashing ocean flowing in
And out again. And, penitent for sin,
My skin is thin, and tight, and washed with tears.
And when I eat, I catch a fish or two.
No more than that. I must remember You.

3

I know the least, most salt-encrusted rock
Which ever pokes above the pulsing sea.
And every seal and gull is known to me,
Enough to give them names. They are my flock.
I know the grit of every island-stone
That went to build my shelter. I have heard
The raucous tune of every hungry bird,
And all the music of the changing foam.

But I am always silent, so that I
Can be Your ocean and Your endless sky.

4

I made my private desert here. I'll stay
Away from all the world. And I will fall
Into a deeper love of You. I'll crawl
On bleeding knees from stone to stone. I'll pray
From dawn to dawn. And I'll become, at last,
No more than bones wrapped up in monkish rags.
The birds who nest along these ragged crags
Will use my scraps to decorate their nests.
But I won't be there anymore, for I
Will finally be Your sea and endless sky.

The Desert Spirits- this poem was actually written as a modern *rosc,* using the method of Imbas Forosnai. With the exception of a few connecting and concluding lines, these images all spontaneously occurred as "poetic ecstasy" to my half-asleep mind on a long road-trip through the desert. Don't worry, I wasn't the driver.

Storm banks in the distance on the Texas panhandle
Like diagonal mushroom clouds
Whose silent lightning carves fresh slices
Out of a flat, gray future.
Across the border, and we're inside them.
The raindrops snap at us
Like falling monsters,
Biting at the windshield
In a suicidal dive.
And the wind whistles like a machine run amok,
And the clock stops,
And we are lost to time.

Pain can always be endured
If there is a voice to give protest.
Out here there are two voices:
And a void on either side.
She pouts, and cocks her head at him,
And says-
"Why, perhaps next summer,
When my dear gollem-mad father

Turns the Earth into a prison for the goblins."
"No, my dear," he says. She hasn't understood.
Pain can always be endured
If there is a voice to give protest,
But what I saw there in front of me
Had no mouth, just smooth skin.

The desert mountains are like great bodies
Pockmarked by scrubs,
Pale and obese in their roadside resting places,
As if we were passing
Through a plague pit
Choked with giants.
There's a void on either side of me,
And an unexpected ache.
I am attached to my head like a balloon on a string.
Hours pass in a ghost phase,
Between sleep and waking.
My eyes squint at the mountains
And they become glass
In atomic heat.
Would you know how to find me here?
Would you trade my hope for new memories?
Because the Mojave is mighty
And I don't want to come home.

Great rocks in the distance like the Gods of Stonehenge,
Standing in a circle with an untold secret,
Weaving out our past years
Among scrub brush and sand.
Canyon Diablo is skull dry,
And I hear things I can't remember.
The spirits of the desert
Will trade bone marrow for wisdom:
Parasites of the empty places,
Sleep and learn, sleep and learn.

I found these voices in the wasteland,
Inside a fluttering darkness,
In all the endless, bright ages
Since I last saw your face.
If I could I would call to you,
I would cut your name through this emptiness,

But I'm trading blood for new memories
And I must meet them alone.

Out here the nighthunters
Have long faces and teeth like canine's.
The windmills on the hilltops
Look like arrows in a dragon's spine.
If you would throw dice
With the desert spirits
You must have skin
That drinks everything,
Ready to cough up a basilisk
Close your eyes,
Cut your mouth,
And sing.

Would you know how to find me here?
Would you trade your bones for new memories?
Because there is nothing around me now
But this bright, empty
Faith:
Stretching out, filling everything
Burning atoms
To angel's wings
Killing hearts
Till they break
And sing
And I don't want to come home.

About the Author- Christopher Scott Thompson is the president of the Cateran Society, and the author of several books on the historical Gaelic martial arts. Under the name C.S. Thompson, he is the author of the Noctiviganti dark fantasy novels. Under the religious name of Gilbride or "Servant of Brighid," he has been active in the pagan community for a number of years, serving as the vice president (and briefly the president) of Imbas, a board member of the Fellowship for Celtic Tradition, a flamekeeper of Ord Brighideach and now the Cauldron Cill, and a member of the Kin of the Old Gods temple. He lives somewhere between this world and the Sidhe in the company of his wife Cicely and daughters Leila and Rowan.

Printed in Great Britain
by Amazon